MIDLIFE,

MADNESS,

OR MENOPAUSE

Does anyone know

what's normal?

Patricia J. Richter and Roger Duvivier, M.D.

Library of Congress Cataloging-in-Publication Data

Richter, Patricia J.
  Midlife, madness, or menopause: does anyone know what's normal?/ Patricia J. Richter and Roger Duvivier, M.D.
          p.   cm.
  Includes bibliographical references and index
  ISBN 1-56561-059-8 $12.95

  1. Menopause--Popular works.
  2. Middle aged women--Health and hygiene.
  I. Duvivier, Roger, 1945-   . II. Title

        RG186.R53 1995   95-7134
        612.6'65--dc20   CIP

Edited by Donna Hoel
Cover design: Garborg Design Works
Text Design: Liana Raudys
Printed in the United States of America

Published by
CHRONIMED Publishing,
P.O. Box 59032
Minneapolis, MN 55459-9686

DEDICATION

To Mom,

whose golden years

were tarnished for want of this information.

ACKNOWLEDGMENTS

This book represents a true team effort and could would not have been written without a host of helpers, loved ones, and supporters.

Special thanks go to very special people: to my sisters, Donna Hoel and Judy Wees, who share genes, jokes, and aunts in the attic and who searched for information to help us understand this madness; to Edna Duvivier, who in the face of personal turmoil still had time for words of encouragement; to Harry Richter who weathered mood swings, frustration, and innumerable angry outbursts and never lost his cool or his ability to encourage, and to our daughters, Janie, Hillary, and Beth, who deserve to know more than we did.

Thanks also to Deanna Muehlberger, who always inspires us to do our best—because she always does; to Patti and Emily Gibbons, who energize everyone with their courage and support; and to Sandy Cwik, who keeps the hearth homey and the work environment healthy. We especially appreciate the support and understanding given by Jean Mabee and the wise women of Sebastian and Jo Gabrielson and the women of Weight Watchers International. Thanks also to Ginny Harms for manuscript review and suggestions, to Jolene Steffer and Lisa Tubach for copy editing and proofreading, and to Janie Stidman and Nancy Nelson for friendship and encouragement.

Finally, thank you to all the groups who gave us ideas and reacted to ours: the women of the Minnetonka (Minnesota) Symphony Chorus, the wives and friends of the Apollo Chorus of Minneapolis, Pat Aafedt and her Wisewoman Network, and the staff of Chronimed Publishing.

TABLE OF CONTENTS

Prologue . . . . *ix*

Foreword *1*

Introduction *5*

Chapter 1. Now That I'm Here, Where Am I? *9*

     • What's Happening in Your Body? *11*

     • Helping Yourself Feel Better 16

Chapter 2. What Can You Expect? *21*

     • Symptoms: From Aching Joints to Zits *25*

Chapter 3. The Hormone Express: Will We Ride Forever? . . . *125*

     • What We Know About HRT *125*

     • What We Don't Know About HRT *129*

     • What If You Can't Take Hormones? *137*

• Supporting Your Body *140*

• Hormones Currently Available (chart) *142*

Chapter 4. Hysterectomy: Why and When? *145*

    • How are Hysterectomies Performed? *150*

    • Who Needs a Hysterectomy? *151*

          Fibroids *151*

          Endometriosis *153*

          Dysfunctional uterine bleeding *154*

          Genital or uterine prolapse *156*

    • Other Reasons for Hysterectomy *158*

    • Before You Say Yes to Hysterectomy *159*

    • What Happens After Surgery? *163*

    • What's the Bottom Line? *165*

    • For More Information *166*

Chapter 5. Living Healthfully Ever After *169*

    • What Tests Do You Need? *172*

    • Other Health Concerns. *174*

          Cancer *174*

          Osteoporosis *183*

Heart disease and stroke *188*

Alzheimer's disease *192*

New evidence about vision *194*

• What About Sex? *194*

• What Are You Doing the Rest of Your Life? . . . *196*

Chapter 6. Food for Thought *199*

• Food and Aging *200*

• Where Do We Get Antioxidants? *201*

• Making Changes *202*

• Figuring Out Fats *203*

• Hints for Healthful Eating *204*

• Gaining Weight *205*

• Expected Weight Ranges (table) *206*

• Losing Weight *207*

• More About Calcium *208*

• Phytochemicals *209*

Chapter 7. Reclaiming Your Passion *213*

• Everything's Coming Up Roses *214*

• Put On a Happy Face *216*

- Sleeping With the Enemy 217
- More Tips for Managing Your New Life 220

Chapter 8. Planting the Tree of Knowledge 223
- Menopausal Symptoms Journal 224
- Charting the Family Tree 228
- Madness: Another View 228
- Keeping It in Perspective 233

Bibliography 235
Index 239

$\mathcal{P}$ROLOGUE

It all started in Atlanta—where none of us lives. We were five couples, all old friends spending an evening at a mystery dinner theater and having a great time. We all took part in the drama unfolding before us with little or no self-consciousness. It was a relaxed, friendly, comfortable group.

The play ended, and we waited for dessert. Suddenly, one of us, Nancy, had an anguished, almost tortured look on her face. She fled the table, followed by Alice. Fifteen minutes later, when neither had returned, Carol left to see if help was needed. It was almost another half hour before Pat went after the other three. I remained with the baffled husbands.

The manager now wanted to close for the night, so I was sent to find the missing women. The hideout was obvious—the ladies' room, of course. The scene inside was dramatic, however. Nancy was leaning against the black marble vanity, head back, face to the ceiling. Her eyes were covered with huge wads of brown paper towels. She was flushed, trembling, and damp with perspiration. The other three women were hovering solicitously. The room was filled with mirrors that made the gathering seem larger than life.

"She thought she was losing it—going crazy," Alice volunteered. "She got hit with a hot flash, itching, and an overwhelming need to cry all at once. And since she's only 42, she had no idea what was happening."

We exchanged stories and tried to comfort Nancy, but we actually got ourselves pretty worked up about the injustice of it all. Suddenly the restaurant manager was pounding at the door.

"Leave us alone," Alice shouted, rather uncharacteristically. "We're having an important support group meeting in here."

Thus our idea was born. None of us had any notion of what lay ahead for us as "midlife women." We needed some advice on what to expect, on what is normal. Or at least we wanted to know about some of the stuff that wouldn't be considered grossly abnormal.

And so we began hunting for every piece of information out there. We would all share concerns and ideas, and Pat would do the writing. Roger Duvivier, a caring and concerned physician, teacher, and friend, agreed to supply the latest information and check out the facts. The result is this book, which we hope will help you be more comfortable with the normal ups and downs during these confusing years.

Donna Hoel, Editor

$\mathcal{F}$OREWORD

by *Roger Duvivier, M.D.*

$\mathcal{T}$he traditional concept of the menopause has become outdated and obsolete in my view. I believe it is time to stop talking about "the" menopause and instead focus on the necessary steps to prepare for healthful and graceful aging. All contemporary mature women and those who love them need to prepare for that full third of life that follows menopause. Therefore, in this book, we have chosen to talk not just about menopause, but about independent, intelligent, menophobia-free aging—aging with dignity.

Women can now expect to live beyond the age of 80 and may spend at least a third of their lives in a postmenopausal state. The biological, physical, emotional, psychosocial, and financial implications of these 30 to 40 years spent in an estrogen-deficient state are significant. And while the topic was once taboo, menopause has come of age. It is in the best interest of all women to learn about menopause and to prepare for it and deal with it, armed with the best available knowledge.

The need for good, reliable, scientific, evidence-based data on menopause continues to grow. The more we learn, the more we need to know. More and more women appreciate that the lack of medical research and insufficient scientific information can be or is hazardous to our health. Furthermore, it has become politically correct to plan for the menopause years and for all those years beyond it. Such preparation is also perceived as being healthier for our minds, our bodies, and our psyches.

Women are well aware that menarche, sex, pregnancy, childbirth, and all the phases of a woman's reproductive life are not diseases. Neither is menopause. It has, sadly, taken us longer to accept that aging is not a disease either. A new concept in medical thinking has led to the idea that the symptoms of aging can be kept "subclinical." That is to say, even if many of the symptoms of illnesses that often accompany aging are not totally preventable, they can at least be delayed.

This new idea is leading medical researchers to work toward the concept called "compression of morbidities," that is delaying all symptoms, infirmities, and diseases until the last few months after our 99th birthday, or at least to the last week of that final year of life, after which we all will die quickly, suddenly, and with dignity after a brief, pain-free illness.

Toward this end we hope doctors in general and gynecologists in particular will remain advocates for women's health and help women age gracefully by promoting good health habits and emphasizing wellness. Then, perhaps most women can run out of life before they run out of health—at 105 or 115.

But, we wonder, are health-care practitioners and women learning about menopause from reliable sources? Will this generation of women be able to deal with the postmenopausal years more healthfully than previous generations? The unfortunate reality is that women and their doctors often are not very well informed about menopause. Nor do they share the same sources of information. In fact, a "menopause information gap" seems to have developed.

Women, for example, tend to be concerned about menstrual flow, urinary tract problems, difficulty with concentration, short-term memory loss, hair loss, and the like. Doctors, on the other hand, focus on the science behind the symptoms, such as the pathophysiology of hot flashes or the endocrinopathy of hormonal changes. Doctors tend to believe women are not well informed about menopause and women believe their doctors have no usable information to help them through this no longer silent passage.

For this reason, we offer this informative book. While not a medical treatise on the topic, it should help to answer some questions while it enables you to pose others to discuss with your doctor. One thing has become clear to medical science: Being in a state of estrogen deficiency is not normal, even though many of the symptoms experienced during this time are normal. We hope to help you find out what you can expect if, during your voyage, you do pass from ovarian activity to a state of estrogen deficiency.

The challenge ahead is to work with your doctor to find out the extent of deficiency in your body and to plan for the various therapies that can help you enjoy the rest of your life. You can plan to remain active physically, emotionally, socially, sexually, spiritually, and intellectually. Your sense of usefulness and purpose will be enhanced by continued good health.

One final word: We have not yet learned everything there is to know about the complexities of the female body. Far from it! We know just enough today to be able to prescribe hormone replacement or additive therapy with confidence for many sufferers of hormone deficiency or insufficiency. But we don't yet know the optimum dosages or delivery methods for each woman. For that reason, you'll want to use this book as your introduction to the topic. Then search out more information that will help you live on healthfully and hopefully.

I believe it is the absence of hope that makes us old. If you believe you can no longer control or change your life, you will become old very quickly. This book tells you how much there is to hope for. Those of you who remain "neither shy nor retiring" will discover the fountain of age and continue to grow. For all of us, we hope and we believe the best is yet to be.

INTRODUCTION

Aside from being one of the hot topics on the talk show circuit, menopause is a perfectly normal event that occurs in the lives of all women. The time in a woman's life from ages 35 to 45 is usually called the premenopausal or perimenopausal period, and the time that just surrounds the end of your periods is called the climacteric.

Natural menopause actually means the normal, spontaneous cessation of menses, or the stopping of your periods. The word *menopause* is based on the Greek words that mean "to cease" and "month." You sometimes hear this time referred to as "the change of life." The perimenopause is the time when a woman's ovaries begin producing fewer eggs and less and less of that crucial female hormone, estrogen.

Estrogen plays an important role in women's bodies. It is responsible for the development and maintenance of the female reproductive system. It prepares a woman's vagina for sex. Along with progesterone, it prepares the uterus for embryo implantation. If pregnancy does not occur, the uterine lining sheds through the process called menstruation.

For many women, the decline in estrogen production happens gradually, with periods becoming more irregular between the ages of 45 and 55. Today the average age of menopause is around 51 years. Of course, if a woman has had her ovaries removed surgically, menopause will begin at that time. If the uterus is removed but the ovaries are preserved, a woman will no longer menstruate, but she will not have menopausal symptoms either—at least not until ovarian functions decline.

As her estrogen levels drop, a woman may experience physiological changes. The most widely reported of these is the "hot flash," a flushing sensation like blushing that makes you feel hot from the waist up. Night sweats are also likely to occur.

Some women report waking up in the middle of the night soaked in perspiration and feeling superheated. These episodes can be particularly bothersome since they disrupt sleep and leave you feeling exhausted. Irritability, disorientation, and memory loss may develop as consequences of estrogen deficiency.

Other symptoms include vaginal dryness, headaches, muscle and joint pains, weight gain, dizziness, general lack of energy, irritability, bouts of anger, depression, and loss of sexual drive. Even carpal tunnel syndrome and some forms of arthritis have possible links to menopause.

Sounds pretty gruesome, doesn't it? Well, the news isn't all bad. It's important to remember that until this century, not many women lived much beyond their child-bearing years. Women in the Roman Empire died at 25. By 1500, women only lived to age 35.

In the 1990s, the average life span for a woman is 78 years. This means we now have a full third or more of our lives to live after menopause. And there can be a new-found quality of life during these years that we were unable to enjoy before. For our granddaughters, the prospects are even greater. The baby girl born in the year 2000 can expect to live to age 85.

For many women, menopause is liberating. It means no more risks of unwanted pregnancy and no more periods. For others, this time of life can bring new opportunities for travel, education, or personal development. There are lots of things to look forward to after menopause.

WHAT SHOULD YOU EXPECT?

Menopause is a unique experience for each woman. That's part of the reason why it has taken such a long time to get good information about it. Some women breeze through this time without a single hot flash. Others find they need medical intervention to help them cope with the symptoms. Your own experience will vary from your best friend's. But talking about it and learning about other women's experiences is a great help for most of us.

This book is your introduction to possible changes you might notice. The list is long—possibly even a bit overwhelming. By discussing most of the changes we've heard about, we hope to alleviate fears you might have about what's happening to you.

A word about madness. Most of us probably have a Great-Aunt Ida who went to her room at age 45 and wasn't seen much over the next ten years. "It's her change," our mother whispered—well out of range of any menfolk. "Happens to most women. She just gets a little nutty. Best to stay out of her way."

Oh, great! Another "female problem" to look forward to. Personally, my sisters and I always thought there was a method to this particular case of madness. Great Uncle Henry tried to make Ida feel better by buying her furs and diamonds. But, interestingly, it didn't work. She never did really feel good again, even though she lived another 35 years.

Fortunately, the madness myth has largely been dispelled—we hope. If we behave as if we're crazy, we've probably earned the right. But sometimes the old fear rises, and we wonder if full-blown mental illness is lurking.

We can't get rid of that feeling for you, but we can encourage you not to take yourself and your situation too seriously if you think you're headed to the looney bin. To help you overcome those negative thoughts, we've peppered this book with our personal brand of "madness."

Humor can be a great stress reliever and healer. So go ahead and laugh if you're tempted (we hope) and remember you're not alone with your fears or confusion. Millions of women are going through the very same thing. We just have to get them together to figure out what to do next. This book is one small step. Please share it with your friends.

CHAPTER I

Now that I'm here, Where am I?

If you are between the ages of 35 and 45, you're probably at least a little curious about the big M—menopause. While the average age of menopause is actually 51 or 52, depending on the expert reporting it, there are some very important things you need to start thinking about at around age 35 if you want to assure yourself the most comfortable perimenopausal and postmenopausal years possible.

The actual signs of menopause, including hot flashes and night sweats, can begin as early as age 35. Also, bone loss seems to start at around age 40, and no one is exempt. For some women, though, lack of information about the symptoms of menopause leaves them really confused about what's going on.

Barb worked with and loved horses all of her adult life. She owned a couple, spent most of her time at the barn, and taught riding. Then suddenly she found herself allergic to her horses. She couldn't tolerate being around them; she became very nauseated. She couldn't even stand the smell. Yet she continued to love her animals. What a dilemma!

In addition to losing her tolerance for her horses, she became allergic to hay and had to stay away from the barn altogether. She had just turned 40 and now the best days of her life appeared to be over. Oh, yes, she had a husband and a family, and she tried to get involved as passionately at home and at her son's school as she had been with her horses. But fatigue prevented her from doing so. She also felt depressed most of the time. She believed that it was the loss of her great love, her hobby, that brought her down.

Barb had always had trouble with her periods. Now they became sporadic and even more unpredictable. The intervals between periods would lengthen, and then she'd have two periods only a week apart. Her doctor told her she was experiencing some classic symptoms of severe stress. She continued to believe this was all due to her inability to enjoy her horses. And she felt more and more exhausted.

Barb began to wake up at night. She'd find herself soaking wet, and she'd feel so much anxiety that on more than one occasion she had her husband rush her to the emergency room. Accompanying her feelings of panic were heart palpitations that convinced her she was having a heart attack.

You probably have enough clues by now to know that Barb was entering the perimenopause and experiencing hormonal shifts that triggered her strange problems. Sadly, Barb didn't have a clue as to what was happening—and neither did her doctor.

It would be less than honest to report that Barb started hormone therapy and got her old life back. She didn't. She started the therapy, and she continued to work toward restored good health, but it didn't happen overnight. It usually doesn't.

Barb's tolerance for horses did get better, but for some reason many of the allergies were slow to resolve. In her case, long-term exposure to substances her body was sensitive to affected her immune system. Fixing the immune system is more difficult than managing menopause. But it is important to note that some symptoms of one mimic the other. And it is also interesting that the onset of the allergies was the tip-off that she was entering the perimenopausal period.

WHAT'S HAPPENING IN YOUR BODY?

Here's a lot of information about how your body works, things you didn't even know that you didn't know. Most are things your mother never told you, simply because she didn't know them either. Yet they are things you probably should know as you approach menopause.

All women are born with all the eggs their ovaries will ever release. Until puberty, most eggs lie dormant. When menstrual periods start, a cyclic process begins that continues for most of a woman's adult life.

With each period, some women have mood changes; some retain water and experience swelling of breasts, hands, or feet; and some suffer backaches, headaches, and depression. For many women, however, menstruation is not uncomfortable. And lots of women thoroughly enjoy their role in the propagation of the human species.

However, for women for whom contraception has been an ordeal or whose reproductive systems never worked exactly right, menopause is anticipated with more joy than motherhood was. Some women even opt to induce sudden menopause by undergoing hysterectomy long before ovarian function stops or a medical need mandates it.

Moments of Madness

•

OUR FAVORITE BUMPER STICKERS:

HONK IF YOU'RE RETAINING WATER!

I BRAKE FOR ESTROGEN!

While all women experience cycles of reproductive fertility and monthly bleeding, few women fully understand the process itself. Each woman passes through a series of phases each month of her life. Each phase leads into another phase creating the monthly cycle.

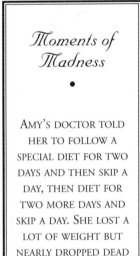

Moments of Madness

•

AMY'S DOCTOR TOLD HER TO FOLLOW A SPECIAL DIET FOR TWO DAYS AND THEN SKIP A DAY, THEN DIET FOR TWO MORE DAYS AND SKIP A DAY. SHE LOST A LOT OF WEIGHT BUT NEARLY DROPPED DEAD FROM ALL THAT SKIPPING!

Here's how we think it works. A part of the brain called the hypothalamus sends a biochemical prompt to the pituitary gland telling it to release certain chemicals. One of these chemicals is called follicle stimulating hormone or FSH. This FSH is what causes some of the follicles in the ovaries to begin to swell. This, in turn, leads to the maturation and release of an egg. Why a particular egg is selected for maturation is still a mystery.

As the follicles ripen, they also release estrogen. The estrogen, in turn, sends a signal back to the brain that it is time to turn off the FSH. As estrogen levels in the blood rise, the pituitary is stimulated to release another chemical called luteinizing hormone (LH), which tells the follicle to open and shed the egg. The estrogen also prompts the uterus to rebuild its lining.

Obviously the process is not as simple as our description. Nor is ovarian activity the only source of estrogen production in women. Estrogen comes in several forms. One, estrone, remains fairly constant, while another form, estradiol, fluctuates widely.

After ovulation, the ovarian follicle is converted to a yellow matter, called the corpus luteum. This in turn secretes progesterone, the hormone that supports pregnancy. Progesterone acts on the lining of the womb, causing it to thicken, accumulate blood vessels, and provide the right conditions for an implanted fertilized egg. The combination of progesterone and estrogen is also the chemical signal that tells the brain to reduce the production of both FSH and LH.

If the egg remains unfertilized, the secretion of estrogen and progesterone ceases; the womb lining begins to drop away, to be shed and flushed out with blood. In the absence of estrogen and progesterone, the hypothalamus starts up again, sending out FSH and LH, and the cycle begins again. At menopause these interlocking processes begin to slow down and misfire.

It all sounds pretty complex—because it is! We still have a lot to learn about the way the female body works. Research on menopause, which affects the long-term health of half our human population, was once considered too expensive to pursue. Time and money was spent on more clearly defined life-threatening diseases. Menopause was hardly considered life threatening, let alone a disease. It was and is a normal, if somewhat unpredictable, part of every woman's life.

Experts believe decreases in estrogen cause many of the changes that lead to menopause. The process is not a uniform one; the old mechanism often runs on irregularly under some mysterious momentum. We have very little information about what is happening to the relationship of the hypothalamus, the pituitary, and the ovary during the perimenopause when menstrual patterns begin to change. The ovaries are believed to run out of follicles, produce less estrogens, and ovulate less regularly.

Today the average woman is fertile for about 30 to 40 years. Her hormonal cycle may begin to change when she reaches her mid-thirties, however, and her fertility may diminish. Not only does she have fewer eggs, but the follicles that remain are less sensitive to hormonal stimulation. Some months, one follicle may be stimulated enough to mature and release an egg. Other months, no ovulation occurs.

This stage of a woman's life is described as the perimenopause. At this time, menstruation may occur more or less often and be heavier or lighter than normal.

Without the release of an egg during ovulation, progesterone, which depends on the corpus luteum for production, is no longer secreted. Although estrogen levels drop too, the ovaries, adrenal glands, and fat cells are still able to provide some estrogen. As a result, the uterine lining is stimulated exclusively by estrogen. It continues to grow until it lacks a sufficient blood supply. When this happens, the woman will possibly miss one or two periods, but when the endometrium is finally shed and menstruation begins, the period may be much heavier than normal.

At about this time, women may experience some of the signs and side-effects associated with decreases in hormones, such as hot flashes and night sweats. In the meantime, however, the hypothalamus and pituitary glands continue to release FSH and LH in their futile attempt to stimulate ovarian activity. Because of this, FSH and LH levels can be used to determine if a woman has entered the perimenopausal years, the time leading up to menopause. FSH levels can reach 13 times normal and LH levels often triple during this time.

Eventually the few remaining ovarian follicles no longer respond to hormonal prodding, ovulation stops, ovarian hormone levels drop further, and a woman stops menstruating altogether. Menopause is usually considered "official" once a woman has gone for a full year without menstruating.

During the perimenopausal years, hormonal changes occur not only in your ovaries but also in your adrenal, thyroid, pancreas, pineal, and pituitary glands. A visit to an endocrinologist during this period may provide a two fold benefit.

First, you will get an overall and perhaps less confusing picture of your hormone levels and learn if estrogen depletion is occurring. Second, you can contribute to building the knowledge base by helping medical science discover what is a "normal" level of the various hormones your body produces.

It is important to know that almost every part of your body is changed, however subtly, by the levels of estrogen and progesterone your ovaries are producing. All of the sex organs, both inside and outside of the body, need estrogen to work properly.

Moments of Madness

•

"DO YOU AND YOUR HUSBAND HAVE MUTUAL ORGASM?" THE YOUNG WOMAN ASKED.

"NO," REPLIED HER OLDER COMPANION. "I THINK WE HAVE STATE FARM."

One of the key challenges to defining appropriate hormone replacement therapy is the lack of knowledge about hormone levels before estrogen depletion. Since the 1980s, the therapeutic approach has been standardized. Women usually start with pills containing 0.625 milligrams (mg) of conjugated estrogens or 1 mg of estradiol, or with a skin patch of 0.05 mg of estradiol. Each woman thus undergoes an experimental phase during which her symptoms are the only indicators of whether she is getting enough or too much estrogen.

HELPING YOURSELF FEEL BETTER

Starting at age 35, your diet becomes particularly important in helping you feel your best. We women generally believe the adage, "You can never be too thin or too rich." We can't comment on the rich part, but there is now some evidence that you really can be too thin.

Heavier women tend to have higher levels of estrogen for longer periods of time than thin women, and this seems to be associated with fewer problems with menopause. Also, thin women are more vulnerable to rapid bone loss and consequently tend to have more fractures and breaks.

Starting around age 35, women tend to have difficulty losing extra pounds. This may be because the body, sensing a slow down in estrogen production, wants to create more fat cells in which to store estrone, a natural form of estrogen. Awareness of what is happening can help a lot at this time.

Your body is in a constant flux of death and regeneration. Every day some cells die and others are recreated to replace them. Every day, your heart beats, your food is digested, and your senses let you see, smell, and make contact with your world. The catalyst for all these processes is the nutrient content of the foods you eat.

At different times of your life your body requires special ingredients to perform special functions. During the transitional years surrounding menopause, calcium-rich foods should be a high priority to protect you from osteoporosis, heart disease, and even emotional swings.

If you are perimenopausal, you need at least 1,000 mg of calcium per day. After menopause, you need 1,600 mg daily. While there is not much information available about exactly how much calcium you should get in your youth to prevent osteoporosis in your later life, there is evidence that American women are sadly lacking in calcium in their diets. The average woman in the U.S. between the ages of 45 and 65 is only getting 460 to 650 mg daily, less than half of what her body requires for bone maintenance.

As women grow older, the balance among the various food groups—carbohydrates, proteins, and fats—the calories consumed, and the nature and amount of exercise become increasingly important. While good nutrition is the natural pathway toward healthy bone, remember that bone requires a healthy foundation of protein. It is into this protein that minerals, especially calcium, are deposited.

In combination with a healthy diet, exercise plays a major role in premenopausal well-being. A commitment to daily exercise goes a long way toward ensuring a healthier, independent life in the years ahead.

Weight-bearing exercise (such as walking, running, and cross-country skiing) can play an important role in preventing osteoporosis. To avoid this devastating illness, women should try to develop as much bone mass as possible before menopause. Reducing the rate of bone loss that occurs during menopause is also important.

Inappropriate diet, lack of exercise, and smoking all promote bone loss. Moderate exercise is particularly beneficial. When carried to extremes, exercise causes problems for some women, both because of injuries and because of loss of too much body fat.

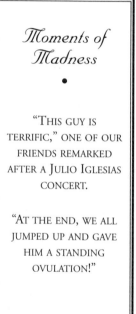

Moments of Madness

•

"THIS GUY IS TERRIFIC," ONE OF OUR FRIENDS REMARKED AFTER A JULIO IGLESIAS CONCERT.

"AT THE END, WE ALL JUMPED UP AND GAVE HIM A STANDING OVULATION!"

One of the biggest problems with exercise programs is "poor compliance." That is, we want to do it, but we hate to do it, so we just don't do it. But for the sake of present and future health, the healthiest approach is "just do it."

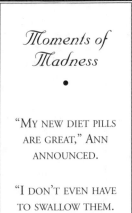

Moments of Madness

•

"MY NEW DIET PILLS ARE GREAT," ANN ANNOUNCED.

"I DON'T EVEN HAVE TO SWALLOW THEM. THREE TIMES A DAY I SCATTER THEM ACROSS THE FLOOR AND THEN PICK THEM UP."

You're probably sick to death of hearing about the virtues of exercise. Still, most of us know that women who exercise regularly look better, have more self-confidence, and have more energy than those who don't. This aura of health and well-being is a direct result of flexibility, strength, and improved oxygenation that come from regular exercise.

Studies have shown that supplemental calcium and vitamin D help maintain healthy bone, but unless you exercise, they do little good. According to Dr. Wulf Utian, a recognized menopause expert, you need to establish the following goals for your exercise program.

EXERCISE TO:

- Make your heart and lungs more efficient
- Strengthen and tone your muscles
- Improve your muscle endurance
- Increase your flexibility

To meet these goals, try exercise that is both aerobic (that is, it works your heart and lungs) and weight-bearing (to build your muscles, increase your flexibility, and promote healthy bones).

Examples of aerobic exercise include walking, running, jogging, swimming, and dance programs designed to use oxygen. Weight-bearing exercises are those that work against gravity and include walking, cycling, golfing, playing tennis, dancing, and weight-lifting.

Some studies have shown that weight-bearing exercises and muscle contractions work together to generate stress on the bone that is vital to preventing bone loss. Today many women are pumping iron using free weights, barbells, and weight disks to increase and maintain bone health.

How much you should exercise depends on your current level of fitness. Always start a new exercise program slowly. Soreness or injury sets you back and is a greater deterrent to achieving fitness than taking it slowly and steadily.

You should plan to exercise four times a week for 20 to 45 minutes per session. When you decide which exercise is right for you—something you enjoy—make a regular date with yourself to do it.

CHAPTER II

WHAT CAN YOU EXPECT? FROM ACHING JOINTS TO ZITS

We wish we could tell you exactly what's normal for a woman nearing or already in menopause. The fact is, there is no such thing as normal. Symptoms vary widely from one woman to the next. Nonetheless, there are many changes or symptoms that are relatively common in women in midlife. We'll tell you what we can about these symptoms and offer some options for dealing with them.

What follows is a menopause symptom index developed by Dr. Phillip Sarrel of the Yale School of Medicine in New Haven, Connecticut. The index lists the most frequently reported symptoms and ranks them in terms of their frequency. The resulting score gives you and your doctor a measurement of changes from visit to visit and can help to assess your progress if you decide to start hormone replacement therapy. Take this form with you to your doctor to discuss where you stand on your passage through menopause.

This list is also a valuable tool for you to record information to share with your daughters. By using the questionnaire and the lists to write down your unique experiences, you'll help the next generation of women in your family know what they might expect when it's their turn.

MENSI MENOPAUSE QUESTIONNAIRE

The following questions should be asked: "In the last month did you experience . . . ?" Indicate by circling the numbered response for the first part of each question.

Code for your answers:

> 0 = No;
>
> 1 = Occasionally;
>
> 2 = Yes, on a regular basis

The reply to the second part of the question, "Is it a real problem for you?" should be indicated by circling Yes or No.

1. Hot/warm flushes (flashes)?	0	1	2
Problem?	Yes	No	
2. Palpitations (heart flutters)?	0	1	2
Problem?	Yes	No	
3. Headaches?	0	1	2
Problem?	Yes	No	
4. Sleep disturbance (insomnia)	0	1	2
Problem?	Yes	No	
5. Chest pressure/pain?	0	1	2
Problem?	Yes	No	
6. Shortness of breath?	0	1	2
Problem?	Yes	No	

7. Numbness?	0	1	2
Problem?		Yes	No
8. Weakness or fatigue?	0	1	2
Problem?		Yes	No
9. Pain, aches in bone joints?	0	1	2
Problem?		Yes	No
10. Memory loss?	0	1	2
Problem?		Yes	No
11. Anxiety?	0	1	2
Problem?		Yes	No
12. Depression?	0	1	2
Problem?		Yes	No
13. Fear of being alone in public?	0	1	2
Problem?		Yes	No
14. Loss of urinary control?	0	1	2
Problem?		Yes	No
15. Vaginal dryness?	0	1	2
Problem?		Yes	No
16. Loss of sexual desire?	0	1	2
Problem?		Yes	No

17. Pain with intercourse?   0   1   2

      Problem?   Yes   No

18. Disrupted function at home?   0   1   2

      Problem?   Yes   No

19. Disrupted function at office?   0   1   2

      Problem?   Yes   No

20. Other symptoms

_____

_____

_____

_____

_____

_____

_____

_____

_____

      Mensi Score (0-38)   _____

      Number of "Yes" Answers   _____

From OBG Management, October 1993, courtesy of Philip Sarrel, M.D., Yale School of Medicine

A more complete list of signs of menopause follows. Those on the Mensi questionnaire are included, but many that are reported less frequently are also listed in this section to help you identify what may be normal for you.

ACHING JOINTS AND MUSCLES

A

(See also Cramps of legs and feet)

Marty has been plagued by aching joints and muscles for months. Her physician tends to dismiss her complaints as imaginary. She really hurts, but no one will tell her why. The tense muscles keep her awake at night, and she has become the victim of a vicious circle of pain and fatigue. Is this normal?

Many women have aching joints and muscles at this time of life—often with good reason. Lifting, exercising, hauling kids, sitting at a desk for too long, getting cold—all can cause muscles and joints to ache. But hormones, too, play a role for some women.

As your body produces less estrogen, many of the tissues of the body begin to dry out. Muscle tissue inside the body is not excepted. The joints are also affected in this drying process. Lowered estrogen levels seem to reduce muscle strength and increase stress on the joints.

Sometimes this pain results in backaches or stiff and sore shoulders. Doctors sometimes label the condition "myalgia," meaning painful muscles. In addition, some women report waking in the night because of leg or foot cramps. For some women, these cramps may be linked with calcium deficiency. Calcium is particularly important to women, not just because of its role in preventing osteoporosis, but because of its critical role in bone health, in general.

If you experience joint pain and muscle aching and cramping, you are not abnormal. Women of varying nationalities report this joint and bone pain during the time surrounding the menopause. In Nigeria, more than 40 percent of the women complain of it, and in Japan, sore shoulders and stiffness is the most commonly reported menopausal symptom.

What can you do about aches and pains?

Helping yourself.—Exercise is always beneficial to maintain muscle strength. If you are already participating in some regular exercise program, keep it up. If not, it's time to begin. Also, increase your intake of leafy green vegetables. Calcium supplements also are helpful for many women.

Using traditional medicine.—If your primary physician is not a gynecologist, he or she may be unaware that these symptoms can be related to the perimenopausal syndrome. This is particularly true if you are younger than 45 or so. You may want to make an appointment with a gynecologist to discuss your aches and pains.

Hormone replacement therapy (HRT) and hormone additive therapy (HAT) are two medical alternatives known to help many women. (There is a complete discussion of hormones in the next chapter.) Estrogen therapy increases blood flow and oxygen in cells and improves the production of joint fluid.

Other possibilities.—For immediate relief, rub the muscles to increase the blood flow, and massage them to reduce the cramps and ease the pain. Some women report that acupuncture helps reduce the pain. Vitamin E also seems to work for some women. Massage therapy can also help and can improve circulation and posture in general.

ACNE

Susan was sitting at her grandson's little league baseball game with her chin in her hands. She was embarrassed at the condition of the skin on her face. It was marred by pimples. She said to her daughter, "I can't believe this; I'm 50 years old and I have more zits now than I ever had as a teenager. I wonder what's going on? I'm not eating chocolate, and I don't pig out on French fries. I must have a glandular disorder. This just can't be normal."

Acne generally shows up during adolescence and often during pregnancy because of changing hormones. So we probably shouldn't be surprised when it flares again during menopause. Many women have blackheads, whiteheads, or inflammatory lesions of some kind on their delicate facial skin around this time. It's a nuisance, but it's not abnormal.

What can you do about acne?

The obvious first step is to keep your face clean. One change you may want to make at this time, though, involves what you use to clean your face. Choose something that doesn't deplete the skin of its moisture, zits or not. Many dermatologists tell women to avoid soap. Read the labels and look for something fortified with vitamin E or A.

Helping Yourself.—In addition to keeping your face clean, you'll want to moisturize your skin. Some dermatologists recommend Retin-A, a form of vitamin A, to clear up acne and nourish the skin. Retin-A is usually available over the counter in various preparations. One of the cautions for its use, however, is to stay out of the sun. Beta carotene, the natural form of vitamin A, is available through the foods you eat. Carrots are a particularly good source.

Using traditional medicine.—Once again, bringing the hormones back into balance usually fixes this skin problem. Read the complete chapter on hormone replacement therapy and hormone additive therapy to better understand your options. Another approach is to see a dermatologist and get prescription medications that will clear up the problem.

If you do get a prescription, it is vitally important—as with all medications, not just those for acne—to follow the instructions. If you are told to use a preparation for 10 days, it is important to do so. Even if the symptoms clear after a day or so, keep taking the medicine for the prescribed time.

Other possibilities.—Once again vitamin E, as a cream, has been considered helpful. A dietary supplement of vitamin A, if you believe you are deficient, is also something to consider. Reevaluate your use of soaps and creams, and read the labels to decide which is best for you. Remember, lotions, whether containing elastin, collagen, or vitamin E, only work on the surface of the skin. They don't heal deeper problems.

ALLERGIES

Cynthia couldn't understand why, when she had been a gardener her entire life, she could spend only an hour in her garden before she had a raging headache. Nothing in her yard had ever bothered her before. She had just turned 48, and suddenly she felt like she was becoming allergic to breathing the air. She worried about serious illness and thought this just couldn't be normal.

While there is no clear evidence about the relationship of allergies to menopause, more women tend to experience environmental or food allergies at midlife than at any other time in their lives. Because science has proved there is a relationship between the strength of the immune system and the hormonal balance in the body, it is fairly safe to conclude that allergies are more likely to appear when the body is in a state of hormonal imbalance.

This is one of the concerns we hope will gain some attention from medical researchers, since the presence of allergies can have a profound impact on a woman's life. Let's face it, if you are ill from a blinding headache, you're not likely to be enjoying any of your regular activities. For some women, allergies become immobilizing.

Environmental allergies can be bad, but food allergies can be dangerous. Many women report that monosodium glutamate or MSG, a substance often found in Chinese food that keeps food looking fresh and colorful, becomes a serious problem.

Wheat has also been reported as a potential problem for many. Allergies don't always appear as sinus aggravations, but can emerge as inflammation of the joints, rashes, and respiratory difficulties, among others.

What can you do about allergies?

The key to managing allergies is to be sensitive to the foods you eat and the environmental elements you confront. If you have respiratory symptoms you've never had before, you probably want to get professional help. Allergy testing can often uncover the cause of your symptoms. However, keep in mind that some signs of allergies in midlife are normal.

In the presence of some specific autoimmune diseases, such as lupus or rheumatoid arthritis, a woman's body may make antibodies that attack her ovaries and destroy the supply of eggs prematurely. We don't know why this happens, but if you have a chronic illness, you want to be sure that your physician or your gynecologist helps you keep track of your ovarian function. You could enter menopause earlier than other women.

Helping yourself.—If you decide against allergy testing and you have some idea of what's bothering you, you can do some experimenting yourself. Suppose you get a headache every time you drink red wine. Try stopping the red wine for at least three days, then drink some and see if the headache comes back.

Moments of Madness
•

"I REALLY CAN'T COMPLAIN ABOUT MY HUSBAND," SAID MARY. "HE'S AN ANGEL."

"OH, I'M SO SORRY," JANE RESPONDED. "I DIDN'T KNOW HE HAD DIED."

Of course, staying away from red wine would be an obvious solution if it turns out to be the culprit. You could experiment with different kinds of red wine. Then test yourself again. You may find that you can tolerate one for a time and then the headache appears again. Then maybe it's time to switch to grape juice.

Whatever the food you suspect, repeat this kind of test. Eliminate the food from your diet, then reintroduce it and pay close attention to your body's reaction. Watch for symptoms and change your diet accordingly.

Over-the-counter antihistamines can help reduce some symptoms, but be careful. During the perimenopausal period, the tissues of your body are drying out. Antihistamines dry them even more.

Using traditional medicine.—If allergies are a serious problem for you, see your doctor or consult a specialist. Continuous environmental allergies can result in more serious problems down the road.

There are a number of nasal sprays that can block various allergens. Pine pollen, for example, can be neutralized before it reaches the lungs. Most of these sprays are available by prescription only, so ask about them. Other prescription antihistamines, like Seldane®, provide relief without causing drowsiness. But don't forget that antihistamines can dry you out in places where you'd rather be moist.

Other possibilities.—Many people are looking at alternative medicine these days, including homeopathic remedies. Essentially, homeopathic remedies are based on the "hair of the dog" theory. That is, taking a little of the substance that causes the problem can be the basis of the cure.

Some allergists and "alternative physicians" can test you for your reactions to various substances. They then prepare individual formulations, usually as drops to be used under the tongue two or three times a day. The formulation is based in part on the allergen.

The theory behind this treatment is that when you have an allergic reaction, your body's immune system works very hard to process or evict (as with a sneeze) the offending substance. If the immune system loses the battle, you become increasingly allergic to that substance and possibly other substances as well.

With a homeopathic formulation, you take small doses of the offending substance to help strengthen the immune system's response to it. This is sometimes compared with exercising a muscle. The more you exercise it, the stronger it becomes. Little by little the immune system adjusts to processing the offender and it no longer causes problems.

More and more conventional allergists are taking a fresh look at the homeopathic approach. In fact, some large clinics now have entire departments of alternative medicine for people who are uncomfortable with standard medical treatment.

ANXIETY

Ellen woke up suddenly. She felt terrified. Her chest was pounding. She rushed into the bathroom, thinking she was going to be seriously sick. She was trembling. Her stomach was churning and she had diarrhea. "What's going on?" she said aloud. "Am I having a heart attack or am I going crazy?"

Ellen was experiencing an anxiety attack. These attacks don't always strike at night, but many times they do. You could be in a shopping mall and suddenly feel short of breath, drained of all your energy, and scared. Or you could be at the movies and suddenly feel like you've got to get out. You're panicky and you feel trapped.

It doesn't sound like any fun, but first of all, try to remember that you are not going crazy. Your body is changing and with this change come certain behavioral aberrations in some women. The anxiety attack is probably one of the most uncomfortable.

What can you do about anxiety?

Sometimes the anxiety you feel is related to real midlife problems. Perhaps your husband is facing retirement and you are worried about this big adjustment. Maybe you just suffered the loss of a loved one. There is likely to be some anxiety as you process these complicated feelings.

If you are between 35 and 60 years old, however, and if you cannot find a psychological trigger for your anxiety, it is quite possible that you are suffering anxiety because of hormonal changes.

Helping yourself.—Be sure to talk to someone about these anxiety attacks. During the perimenopausal period, you are likely to experience many emotional changes. While these may be related to specific circumstances in your life, your ability to deal with them could be impaired because of the hormonal imbalance in your body.

Moments of Madness

•

LUCY: "SHE'S SO ANXIOUS, SHE CAN'T EVEN GO TO A MOVIE. SAYS SHE CAN'T STAND SITTING."

GRACIE: "WHAT'S STRANGE ABOUT THAT? BET SHE CAN'T SIT STANDING, EITHER."

Adrenaline, for example, is a hormone that helps you to escape danger and it sometimes runs amok during this time. The adrenaline flowing through your body may cause you to feel frightened when you really aren't in any danger.

Adrenaline isn't the only culprit. The effects of the various hormones on the brain are complex and defy simple explana tion. Anxiety is something you should discuss with your doctor. If you don't feel comfortable asking your doctor about this, it might be time to shop around for another doctor.

Using traditional medicine.—When the problem is strictly hormonal, estrogen replacement or hormone additive therapy can be very effective in eliminating anxiety attacks. If you are undergoing both a midlife crisis and menopause simultaneously, you may want to consider seeing both your gynecologist and a psychologist or psychiatrist.

Your doctor may want you to use something like Xanax® or Prozac® to help you over the humps. Read everything available about whatever is recommended, and then make the best decision you can with that information. Try not to be too impatient about seeing improvement. Sometimes these drugs take a lot longer to work than we expect.

Other possibilities.—A diet rich in vitamin B_6 is helpful for many women. Foods high in this vitamin include chicken, fish, pork, eggs, unmilled rice, oats, whole wheat, soybeans, peanuts, and walnuts. Eliminating caffeine and alcohol also may help.

Cutting back on sweets may help too, because refined sugar can cause spiking of blood sugar. While sweets make you feel good for a while, they often leave you feeling depressed and tired. Replace sugar with complex carbohydrates like pasta, beans, peas, and grains.

Changing the way you eat can also help. Eating six small meals instead of three larger ones helps maintain uniform levels of blood sugar. This has helped many women feel more calm and in control.

Some reports have indicated that vitamin B_6 is helpful in the management of the symptoms of premenstrual syndrome (PMS), which can also include feelings of anxiety. A word of caution, however. In some people, high doses of vitamin B_6 can cause some neurological symptoms, like tingling in your fingers and toes and numbness. Use good common sense and let moderation be your guide. Never assume that if a little is good, a lot is better.

Here's a quick tip for immediate management of an anxiety attack. Stop what you are doing, find a place to sit down, and begin to breathe deeply. Take air in through your nose, counting to ten slowly, then exhale the air slowly through your mouth, again counting to ten. Repeat this for twenty breaths, then reassess the level of your anxiety, and continue if needed. Concentrate on your breathing, counting slowly and calmly.

BAD BREATH

Jeannie had always been known for her beautiful smile. When she turned that smile on, the room always seemed to light up. Suddenly, however, Jeannie found that people were turning away from her, or their hands would go up to their noses as though they had some phantom itch. She wondered, "What's going on? How can I suddenly have bad breath?"

Jeannie decided to get more information. Her dentist told her she had "gingivitis," an inflammation of the gums. This early, mild stage of gum disease is caused by the bacteria in plaque, the film that continuously forms on teeth and gums. Gingivitis causes a loss of gum where it attaches to teeth, creating what are commonly referred to as pockets. Gingivitis is the precursor to the more serious "periodontal disease." This disease can lead to infection that affects the bony socket of the tooth, with eventual tooth loss.

The bad news about gum disease is that it appears quite frequently in both men and women during midlife. The good news about gingivitis is it's reversible.

Helping yourself.—In addition to working with your dentist or periodontal surgeon to correct the gum disease, you'll want to begin a program of oral hygiene that includes multiple daily brushings and flossings. Plaque-fighting toothpaste and rinses that help keep bacteria in check also work in many cases.

Some other causes of bad breath are much easier to control. Drinking too much coffee is one and can be fixed by cutting back. Sinus infections can also cause a nasty taste and bad breath. Such infections usually require medical attention.

Using traditional medicine.—It was once believed that losing our teeth was an inevitable part of aging. This is simply untrue! The bone loss common after menopause also was thought to be linked with periodontal disease. This is also untrue!

Recent studies have shown no relationship between osteoporosis and the progression of gum disease. Some studies have, however, shown there is a correlation between an increased risk of gingivitis and pregnancy and birth control pills. This is believed to occur because of the hormonal and vascular changes that occur with pregnancy, changes that are mimicked with the use of oral contraceptives.

Regular dental checkups and professional cleanings (every six months) are effective in the prevention of gum disease at every age. X-rays are useful in assessing bone loss, and your dentist can use a tool called a periodontal probe to measure the depth of gum pockets.

Other possibilities.—If you can't brush after every meal and if flossing is difficult for you, there are many products on the market to help. Chewing sugar-free gum after every meal can help to remove food particles from between the teeth. Eating a little parsley at the end of a meal freshens the breath. Breath mints, sprays, and mouthwash also help control the problem, at least on a temporary basis.

Many products are available to help people with these problems, including supersonic toothbrushes and high pressure irrigators that remove food particles around the teeth. Check with your dentist or periodontist about what's best for you.

BLADDER CHANGES AND INFECTIONS

Marilyn excused herself from the dinner table and headed for the ladies' room. She didn't bargain for the painful burning sensation she experienced when she urinated. Nor did she expect that when she returned to the table she would need to immediately excuse herself again because she felt another urgent need to empty her bladder. "This is making me crazy," she thought.

It is perfectly normal during the menopausal years to find yourself visiting the bathroom more often than when you were younger. It is also perfectly normal to need to urinate during the night. You may even find that your body leaks small amounts of urine when you sneeze, cough, laugh, or exercise.

Urinary tract infections (UTIs) are often referred to as bladder infections, cystitis, or urethritis. When bacteria grow in the bladder, the infection causes a burning sensation with urination, a sense of urgency, frequent but miniscule urinations, or incontinence.

These infections are many times more common in women than in men. And it is not unusual for women to have many such infections throughout their lives. They are more frequent at the time around menopause because the loss of estrogen weakens the lining of the bladder, urethra, and vagina, leaving them more prone to injury and inflammation. In addition, the low estrogen levels cause vaginal secretions to become less acid and more alkaline, creating an environment more hospitable to harmful bacteria.

There are other reasons for bladder or urinary problems in midlife that aren't related to menopause. Drinking a lot of coffee or tea increases urination. Diabetes may cause frequent, urgent urination. A kidney obstruction or a suppressed immune system also prompts more frequent infections.

Sometimes infections occur after sexual intercourse because bacteria are pushed into the urethra at that time. A new sexual partner or use of a diaphragm may also increase the risk.

Moments of Madness

•

LENA: "MY DOCTOR TOLD ME TO DRINK A GLASS OF CRANBERRY JUICE AFTER A HOT BATH."

HELGA: "DOES IT WORK?"

LENA: "DON'T KNOW. I'VE NEVER BEEN ABLE TO FINISH THE HOT BATH."

What can you do about bladder infections?

Helping yourself.—The most important measure you can take to prevent infectious microbes from entering your system is to keep your vagina and urinary tract clean and healthy. After a bowel movement, always wipe yourself from front to back to prevent bacteria from entering the vaginal area. Also, bathe daily with a good pH balanced soap in warm, not hot, water. Hot baths can be drying, and delicate tissues need more, not less, moisture.

Wear underwear that breathes. Synthetic fibers trap moisture, air, and bacteria, so cotton underwear is usually best. Wear pantyhose that have a cotton crotch. Douches and sprays can increase the risk of infection, so avoid them or use them cautiously. And DO drink lots of water. Try to drink an 8-ounce glass of water at least every two to three hours. This is the ideal way to flush out the bladder to keep it healthy.

Using traditional medicine.—Always take bladder infections seriously since an unattended infection can lead to serious kidney problems later. See your doctor, and then follow the advice given. Because the kind of bacteria causing the problem could influence the type of drugs needed to treat it, your doctor will most likely want to do a urine culture.

Antibiotics are usually used for infections in the bladder or urinary tract, but these are known to cause another uncomfortable condition—yeast infection. Some doctors recommend using a vaginal antiyeast cream or suppository along with the antibiotics.

If you do not have a bladder infection but are instead experiencing a loss of elasticity of the tissues of the bladder common in menopause, hormone replacement therapy may be the solution. There is some evidence that estrogen plays a role in regulating the nerves in the pelvic organs. When hormone levels change, these nerves may react by making you feel like you have to urinate more frequently.

Other possibilities.—Drinking plenty of fluids, especially plain water, can help prevent bladder infections. When you do urinate, always empty your bladder completely. If you are menstruating, change your tampons or pads often to discourage bacterial growth. Urinating before and immediately after sexual intercourse helps flush bacteria out of the urethra.

Vitamin B and C supplements help many women counteract frequent bladder infections. Also, eating active-culture yogurt can help deactivate harmful substances in the vagina (and provide valuable calcium at the same time). If you take calcium supplements, be aware that they can encourage bacteria to stick to the bladder wall, which may increase your risk of bladder infections.

According to research done at the State University of New York at Stony Brook, the very best thing you can do to counteract bladder problems is always urinate right away when you first feel the urge.

Studies discovered that the biggest difference between women with and without urinary tract problems was that the women with problems always waited about an hour before they urinated. Those who didn't have problems went to the bathroom immediately when they felt the urge.

And then there is cranberry juice! *The Journal of the American Medical Association,* March 1994, reported the results of the first large-scale clinical trial of the use of cranberry juice in the treatment of urinary tract infections. Daily drinks of cranberry juice reduced the frequency of bacterial bladder infections in older women, and the findings suggest that cranberry juice may have some microbiological effect on the urinary tract.

Finally, Kegel exercises can restore pelvic muscle tone, reduce urine retention, and help prevent bladder infections. These exercises are described on page 97.

BLEEDING

(See Heavy Bleeding, Spotting, and Index)

BONE PROBLEMS

When Marion stood up to dance with her husband, she felt her ankle turn just a little. She might even have felt a little snap— more like a "pop" really. As she walked toward the dance floor, she felt a little nauseated from the sudden pain in her right leg. A trip to the emergency room showed a stress fracture in the bone between the knee and ankle. "How can this happen?" she moaned. "I didn't fall; I didn't slip. All I did was stand up!"

In Marion's case, the weakened condition of her bones was the first indication that she was in the premenopausal period of her life. While the most serious bone loss is known to occur after menopause, there is evidence that a diet high in acidic foods and low in calcium also contributes to bone loss. Estrogen also is involved in repair of bones.

When the body is not given enough calcium to meet its requirements, it draws on its stores. The greatest repository of calcium in the body is, of course, bones. Many women are unaware that their calcium needs increase around age 35, and this increased need continues for the rest of their lives.

If you get your calcium from supplements instead of from dairy products or leafy green vegetables, you need to know that vitamin D is necessary for the absorption of calcium. Vitamin D comes from the sun, but if you use a sun block on your skin, you may be short on this vitamin as well as calcium. You might need a vitamin along with your calcium.

What can you do about it?

Helping yourself.—The time to start building good healthy bones is during your teenage years. If you are already past that age, you can still benefit from making some changes in your exercise and diet habits. Including natural sources of calcium in your diet, increasing your intake of calcium-rich foods like yogurt, cottage cheese, and drinking low-fat milk help build bones. Exercising every day also helps.

Bone loss after menopause isn't totally preventable, but it can certainly be slowed down. Here are the basics: If you are a smoker, quit; if you drink a lot of alcohol, now is the time to stop; and if you don't exercise, start. Extremely thin women also are at higher risk, so think about easing up on the "never too thin" rule.

Exercise that promotes bone growth is called "weight-bearing" exercise. Your body automatically builds bones that can handle your body weight. If walking is your exercise, you can increase the weight load by putting weights on your ankles and carrying weights in your hands while you walk. Weight lifting also both a bone-building and muscle-building exercise.

Other weight-bearing exercises include running, tennis, and low-impact aerobics. Experts caution, however, that the benefits of exercise in promoting bone health only occur if exercise is done regularly.

Using traditional medicine.—The effect of hormone replacement therapy (HRT) in protecting bones is widely established. If your bone density is low or low-normal around the time of menopause, you may want to seriously consider HRT as a way to prevent future problems.

Other possibilities.—If you aren't certain about your bone density, you can ask your doctor to schedule you for a bone density scan. This can assess the mass of your skeletal structure and give you some information to help you monitor bone loss. If there is no scanner available in your area, place a mark on the door frame corresponding to your height, just like you did to measure how your children grew. Every six to eight months, remeasure against the mark. If you are losing height, you are losing bone mass.

Calcium supplements offer another option. Supplements that use the term "carbonate" in their names or descriptions typically provide about 40 percent elemental calcium by weight. That means each Tums® tablet, which is made of calcium carbonate and contains about 200 milligrams of elemental calcium, will provide you with 40 percent of that amount, or 80 milligrams.

Caltrate® 600 with vitamin D comes in 600 milligram tablets. This is also a calcium carbonate, so 240 milligrams, or 40 percent, is the actual elemental calcium available. If your goal is 1600 milligrams daily, you need to take quite a few tablets. Supplements are helpful, but you should still try to include lots of calcium-rich foods in your diet. There's a chart of some of these foods on pages 209.

BREAST CHANGES (OR SORE BREASTS)

Diana was trying on a new blouse. "Gosh," she said to the mirror. "Why don't the buttons around the breasts close anymore? I haven't gained any weight." She tossed the first blouse aside and tried on another, then another. "Nothing fits me anymore. I was always a size 12, and now the darts in the blouse are in the wrong place. I wonder what's going on?"

Changes in the breasts do occur throughout life, and these may become more pronounced with the menopause. As a matter of fact, breasts change every month with the normal reproductive cycle. During the second half of the cycle, breast size can increase because of the increase in activity in the glands and the retention of water.

After menopause, the glandular tissue of the breasts shrinks. In thin women breasts become smaller, while fatter women may experience sagging. A loss of elasticity in ligaments that hold the breasts in place further aggravates the tendency of the breasts to droop. The skin of the breasts may become wrinkled and dry, and the nipples become smaller.

What can you do about it?

Helping yourself.—The changes in the breasts are more profound after a surgical menopause with removal of both ovaries. Sagging results from the loss of elasticity and strength of the muscles and ligaments. The only way to prevent the loss of tone in these muscles is to exercise them. This is one of those cases where some weight training can be of benefit. An experienced personal trainer may be a source of advice.

Using traditional medicine.—As with other changes in the body that result from the depletion of estrogen, breast changes can be counteracted to some degree with hormone replacement therapy. But it is important to exercise to promote good posture and to strengthen the muscles, even if you are taking hormone supplements.

Talk to your doctor if you notice changes in your breasts that seem abnormal to you. Breast lumps, for example, can be very serious and may require immediate medical or surgical action.

Other possibilities.—Your risk of getting breast cancer does increase as you get older. Annual check ups, mammograms, and monthly breast self-exams to detect any changes, however subtle, are extremely important.

BURNING MOUTH

When Shirley woke up, her mouth felt hot and dry and had a bitter taste, so she rushed to brush her teeth. She brushed her teeth again after breakfast. Two hours later she wanted to brush her teeth again. Her mouth was burning, and the bitter taste was still there. "My teeth must be rotting out," she thought. "I've never tasted anything quite this bad. What's happening?"

Some women experience a burning sensation, a bitter taste, and bad breath during the menopausal years. This is because the mucous membranes of the mouth undergo changes when estrogen supplies in the body are diminished. Estrogen seems to be an essential lubricant for all the tissues in the body. As tissues in the mouth and nose dry out, they lose their ability to process secretions. The resulting imbalance leaves a bitter taste with a sensation of heat. The heat leads to a burning sensation on the tongue, on the floor of the mouth, on the hard palate, and in the cheeks.

What can you do about this feeling?

Helping yourself.—Shirley's desire to continually brush her teeth is common. You may find that all your body's smells and discharges change during the years around menopause. In addition to good toothpaste and an effective mouthwash, breath mints or citrus-based candies that encourage salivation may help. Drinking lots of water is a high priority. It's a good idea to always have a glass of ice water available, even at your bedside.

Using traditional medicine.—The burning mouth sensation is another one of those classic menopausal symptoms that seem to resolve with hormone replacement therapy. When the body's stores of estrogen are replenished, many of the discomforts caused by hormone deficiency are corrected. Just how much of what occurs is related to estrogen deficiency and how much is a typical part of aging remains a mystery.

Other possibilities.—If you are really bothered by the sensation of burning in the mouth, check with your dentist first. Your dentist may then refer you to your gynecologist or endocrinologist.

Buzzing in Your Head

Jeannette was taking the minutes at her monthly neighborhood watch meeting when she noticed a peculiar buzzing sound. She completely lost her concentration and instead began focusing on the noise. She poked Shirley, who sat beside her, and asked, "Do you hear that?" "What?" Shirley asked. "That buzzing noise." "I don't hear anything," Shirley replied. Jeannette couldn't concentrate on the meeting and suddenly felt very anxious and disoriented.

What Jeannette was hearing is called "mental static." It is believed to be associated with a momentary electrical discharge in the brain.

Although there is no specific information on the origins of this phenomenon, it seems to occur in some women much like headaches occur in others.

An ongoing study at Rockefeller University in New York has demonstrated a relationship between estrogen and brain function. With lowered estrogen levels come fewer synapses, which connect one neural element to another in our brain pathways. It is quite possible that the sensation of buzzing occurs when various neural elements misfire.

What can you do about it?

Helping yourself.—If this happens to you, the first thing to do is reassure yourself that this too will pass. Don't be frightened, but do be alert. If you are in a position to take a break and relax, do so. If not, excuse yourself for a moment while you regain your bearings.

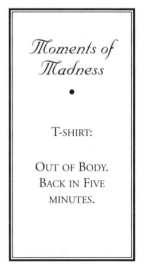

Moments of Madness

•

T-SHIRT:

OUT OF BODY.
BACK IN FIVE
MINUTES.

Using traditional medicine.—For many women, the immediate relief of certain symptoms, like brain static phenomenon, occurs shortly after the start of hormone replacement therapy.

Other possibilities. If you are able to take a break, fix yourself a cup of herbal tea, either chamomile or garden sage with a teaspoon of honey. Both of these herbs are known for their calming effects. In the long run, remember that the buzzing noises will only occur once in a while and will pass relatively quickly.

C

CARPAL TUNNEL SYNDROME

Marianne had a tingling sensation in the fingers of her left hand. It felt like she was being stuck with thousands of tiny pins and needles. The sensation passed, but later her left hand felt numb. And then she began feeling pain.

Marianne was 48 years old. She did not work on computers or typewriters, nor did she keep her left hand in a single position for long periods of time. Still, her doctor said it was probably carpal tunnel syndrome, a disorder of the wrist that mysteriously strikes mostly middle-aged women.

What causes carpal tunnel syndrome?

Dutch researchers have included carpal tunnel syndrome among the symptoms of menopause for some time. They attribute it to "autogenic dysregulation." This involves muscle tone and tension and seems to be related to estrogen.

What can you do about it?

Helping yourself.—When you first become aware of the pins-and-needles sensation, followed by a progressive loss of feeling, take action. Check with your doctor as soon as possible. You may need a specialist.

Using traditional medicine.—As a first course of action, if you are not already on hormone replacement therapy, discuss the possibility of starting with your doctor. Carpal tunnel surgery can be painful and the recovery slow, but if your disease has progressed that far, you may want to consider surgery.

Other possibilities.—You can wear a brace and you can try exercises, but in most cases, carpal tunnel syndrome requires medical attention.

CHEST PRESSURE OR PAIN

(See also Heart Palpitations)

Sandy had just gotten into bed. As she began to relax, she began to feel a tremendous pressure in her chest. Her heart started beating rapidly and she felt panicky. "Oh, my God," she moaned. "I'm having a heart attack." Before she could dial 911, the pressure lightened and her heart rate returned to normal. "Could this be normal?" she wondered.

Sandy's chest pressure and pain with palpitations are relatively common in menopause. These are assumed to be caused by the same vasomotor changes that cause hot flashes. Drops in estrogen apparently trigger spasms of the coronary arteries just as they trigger headaches.

What can you do about it?

Helping yourself.—First, realize this is a fairly common symptom of menopause. Calm yourself, try to relax, and let the feeling pass. Sometimes you'll find the chest pain follows a hot flash; sometimes it precedes one.

Occasionally a racing heart can also occur after too many cups of coffee or after some anxiety-producing experience. As such, it is pretty much harmless and will disappear quickly. The trick is knowing what is harmless and what is not.

Using traditional medicine.—Any recurring heartbeat irregularities and chest pains accompanied by dizziness could signify more serious troubles and should definitely be called to your doctor's attention. For some unknown reason, a phenomenon known as mitral valve prolapse (MVP) occurs more frequently in women than in men (even though the percentages are very small, 5 to 6 percent of women versus 2 to 3 percent of men). But chest pain occurs in 50 to 60 percent of the women with MVP.

If your chest pains don't disappear within a reasonable time (20 to 30 minutes as recommended by the American Heart Association) or if they tend to recur frequently, particularly after you have started hormone replacement therapy, talk to your doctor about having a cardiac workup.

Other possibilities.—The risks for heart disease after menopause are discussed in chapter 5. Because there is no cure for heart disease, prevention is your best defense. If you smoke, quit! If you eat a diet high in fat, don't! If you don't exercise, start! If you like alcoholic drinks, drink only moderately!

CHILLS

Carol woke up in the middle of the night, shaking from chills. "But wait a minute," she thought. "It's 84 degrees in here, and I'm wearing a flannel nightie and socks. Why am I so cold? Is something seriously wrong here?"

With the waning of estrogen in your system come a host of strange symptoms, including elusive "vasomotor disturbances." While the most commonly reported of these is the "hot flash," many women report the opposite effect—chills. Some women have chills right after a hot flash. Both symptoms relate to the activity of your hypothalamus, one of the endocrine glands located in the brain. This gland becomes overstimulated during this time of hormonal imbalance, and you feel the change in body temperature as your blood vessels either contract (as with the chills) or dilate (as with a hot flash).

What can you do to warm up?

Helping yourself.—These chills are legitimate, but they don't mean you're catching a cold. Use blankets, hot water bottles, warm socks, or whatever you need to get comfortable. Drinking hot herbal tea is helpful for some women.

Using traditional medicine.—As with most of the other symptoms of menopause, the chills seem to subside with hormone replacement. It is something to discuss with your doctor.

Other possibilities.—There are other reasons why you might feel chilled: an underactive thyroid, low blood pressure, or other underlying illness. If you have reason to believe there is something else going on in your body, be sure to see your primary physician.

Moments of Madness

•

"MY MOTHER USED TO SAY 'THE OLDER YOU GET, THE BETTER YOU GET, UNLESS YOU'RE A BANANA.' "

—ROSE, ON *THE GOLDEN GIRLS*

CHOLESTEROL, INCREASES IN

(See High Cholesterol)

CRAMPS IN THE LEGS AND FEET

Pat sat up in her bed. The muscles in her legs were cramping, and the cramps were moving down toward her feet. Her groans awoke her husband, who then helped her get up and walk around the room. As the cramps worsened, she lay back down, and he massaged her legs and feet for her. She said, "These are the worst cramps I've ever felt. I sometimes get them in my feet when I change from high-heel shoes to my walking shoes, but I didn't even do that today. This is terrible."

Pat was experiencing an often-reported sign of low estrogen stores. Estrogen keeps muscle tissue supple, and as muscle tissue dries and constricts, cramping can occur.

What can you do about cramps?

Helping yourself.—Massaging the painful area and walking around to relieve the pain is your first course of action. While there is no scientific evidence as yet to support it, some women claim that the use of supplemental vitamin E tablets helps control cramps. Massaging your legs with vitamin E cream may also offer relief.

Using traditional medicine.—Once the hormonal imbalance is restored in your body, leg cramps generally disappear. If hormone replacement isn't an option for you, check with your doctor about other possible treatments.

Other possibilities.—Sometimes cramps are caused by changing the heel heights of your shoes. If you start your day with a one-inch heel, then change to a three-inch, then change to your tennis shoes for your evening walk, you could be setting yourself up for leg cramps.

As you change heel heights, you change the amount of stretch on the calf muscles. This can cause muscle contractions that end in cramps. Try wearing just one heel height for a few days. If you don't get cramps, you can blame your shoes. If cramping still occurs, it could be menopause!

CRAMPS, MENSTRUAL

(See Menstrual Cramps)

CRAWLING SKIN

(See Formication)

CRYING JAGS

Lois was watching TV with her husband when she suddenly burst into tears. "What's wrong?" her husband implored. "Nothing, I don't know what's wrong. I feel out of control and I'm crying. I can't stop," Lois sobbed. She got up, went into the bedroom, and cried herself to sleep.

The "out-of-control" feeling that Lois described is often the basis of a crying jag. Many women find that during the time of the "change," they often feel like crying for no reason at all. Others eventually come to understand they are grieving—for lost loves, unfulfilled goals, even personal slights they haven't thought about for years.

What can you do to control the crying?

Helping yourself.—When you feel like crying, it's probably a good idea to go ahead and cry. If you are in the midst of a crowded office, it's probably pretty unnerving to feel this way. But during this time of hormonal ups and downs, many women report times of sadness. Don't be alarmed, but do be aware of what's going on in your body.

Using traditional medicine.—If you are having crying jags that are part of your menopause, schedule an appointment with your doctor to talk about what's happening. This is yet another case where hormone replacement therapy is known to resolve the symptoms.

Other possibilities.—Of course, if you are grieving for whatever reason—death of a parent or spouse, divorce, or the loss of a job, some crying is normal. But if you find you're immobilized for days by the sadness, talk with someone. A good friend can often be a kindly counsel. Also, read the section about depression on pages 55 to 57.

DECREASED SEXUAL DESIRE

Jack and Cindy had always been passionately in love. They could never remember a time when they hadn't loved each other. Friends since the third grade, they married right after high school. Cindy worked while Jack went to college. They celebrated their 30th wedding anniversary by going to a hotel, drinking champagne, and making mad passionate love, such as they had enjoyed for 30 years.

Now, Cindy lost interest in making love. Jack felt rejected and didn't understand how she could stop loving him when they had been together so long. She couldn't talk about it, because she did not understand it either. She knew she still loved him, but she didn't feel attracted to him. She thought she was losing her mind and even worse, she felt guilty because she was hurting Jack.

Loss of libido, as losing interest in sex is technically called, sometimes occurs during midlife as a result of the hormonal changes taking place in a woman's body. In addition to producing estrogen, the ovaries also produce testosterone, the hormone responsible for your sex drive. Testosterone is also produced in the adrenal glands.

What can you do to increase your interest?

Helping yourself.—Libido isn't totally a matter of the glands. It has often been said that for a woman sexual satisfaction occurs from the neck up. There is some truth to that. For many women, attitude plays a role in determining to whom she is attracted and when. Sometimes as women age, they feel increasingly less attractive and less desirable, which can lead to a loss of libido. Likewise, there may be a tendency to lose interest in sex at midlife because women believe they are expected to stop being interested in sex. If there is any possibility that attitude and beliefs are playing a role, check it out with a good counselor. Talking to someone can often be a major help.

Using traditional medicine.—Just like there are tests to determine your estrogen activity and levels, your testosterone level can be checked. If it is low, you can probably blame hormones for your lost lust. Adding testosterone to hormone replacement therapy is one way to fix the problem.

Other possibilities.—Remember, any major physical illness, disability, or surgical procedure may cause a loss of sexual interest. If you are coping with a chronic illness, you'll want to discuss this with your primary physician. Chronic use of alcohol, tranquilizers, marijuana, or cocaine also affects libido. Depression plays a role as well.

> *Moments of Madness*
>
> •
>
> "I'M AT A PLACE IN MY LIFE WHERE I DON'T CARE WHAT MY HUSBAND WANTS TO DO," ANGIE COMMENTED, "JUST AS LONG AS I DON'T HAVE TO DO IT WITH HIM."

DENTAL PROBLEMS

(See also Bad Breath)

When Sally smiled at herself in the mirror one morning, her teeth looked more yellow than white. She brushed, rinsed, smiled, and brushed again. She also noticed that one of her molars in the back was feeling a little loose, and she thought her teeth looked longer than they used to. "I must be going crazy," she thought. "Certainly teeth don't grow longer. What's up?"

Some changes happen in your mouth by the time you reach midlife. You've probably heard the expression "long in the tooth" referring to age. Gum tissues recede after a half-lifetime of attack from plaque, that sticky, bacteria-laden substance that forms every day. And tooth enamel discolors from coffee, tea, and other foods and drinks.

Drying of muscle tissue and depletion of calcium that affect other body tissues as a result of estrogen deficiency also affect the gum tissue and the jaw bone. Many women who suffer from osteoporosis also have dental problems.

As we age, we produce less saliva, one of the ways our bodies work to counteract plaque in the mouth. Once plaque hardens, it becomes known as tartar, and tartar buildup between the teeth can create pockets that weaken the support for the teeth. The teeth loosen and, without remedial dental work, they may actually fall out.

What can you do to prevent tooth loss and gum disease?

Helping yourself.—For starters, brush after every meal, and floss at least once a day at bedtime. Use tartar-control rinses and toothpastes. Some dentists recommend using an irrigating instrument that massages the gums (like a Waterpik™) to keep tissues healthy.

Watch your diet, and make sure you eat plenty of calcium-rich foods to keep bones and teeth healthy.

Using traditional medicine.—Estrogen again plays a big role in keeping your teeth healthy. Studies have linked osteoporosis of the jaw bone to tooth loss in women after menopause. More women than men wear dentures, but with loss of jaw bone, dentures often do not fit properly. Be sure to tell your doctor about any unusual dental problems that develop. The section on osteoporosis (page 183) contains more information on what to do to combat this disorder.

See your dentist twice a year to make sure tartar is under control. Prevention is your best defense. With daily brushing and flossing and regular check-ups, you and your dentist will be able to catch most problems before they become very serious.

Many women neglect their own care in favor of caring for others, but once you've reached midlife, you really can't afford to not take care of yourself. Gingivectomy, a procedure to repair gum tissue, is performed on women at midlife more than any other surgery.

Other possibilities.—Advances in technology offer a whole new world of solutions to the various dental problems we may have at midlife. With techniques like bonding, we can improve our smiles and whiten or lighten our teeth. If you have already lost some teeth, bridgework may fill the gap.

A relatively new technique called dental implantation has given hope to many women who have faced tooth loss for one reason or another. With implantation, artificial teeth are implanted into your jawbone, providing you with a new smile. While this technique is expensive, it is an alternative to dentures. The best solution? Take care of your teeth and gums so you don't have to consider any of these options.

DEPRESSION

Nan opened her eyes and peered over the blanket. The sun was up, but she didn't care. She thought, "Another day and I feel just as bad as I felt yesterday and the day before that and the day before that. It's all so hopeless. Nothing changes. I don't want to get up, and I don't need to get up, so I won't get up." She burrowed down deeper into the covers. She didn't cry; she just felt numb and depressed—very, very depressed. Worst of all, she was immobilized by the feeling and her only thoughts centered on how to put an end to it all.

Why do you feel so blue during the menopausal years?

Researchers have noticed that estrogen levels rise during pregnancy, then fall quite dramatically after the baby is born. Often women experience what has been termed "post-partum blues" as a result of this drop in estrogen. While the exact mechanism is not yet known, estrogen deficiency and aging have both been linked to changes in brain chemicals—catecholamine and serotonin—thought to influence your sense of well-being.

What can you do about depression?

Depression is characterized by negative thoughts about oneself and the world—with insomnia as a prominent component. If you find that you are dwelling on problems in your life, not sleeping, hiding away in books or television, unable to relate to others, and feeling like packing it in, you are depressed. The good news is there is a lot you can do about it.

Helping yourself.—When sleeplessness and depression become immobilizing, it's very important to take some action. First of all, let someone know what you're feeling. We recommend checking things out with your doctor, but also talk to someone close to you—your mate, your friend, your clergy person.

Any treatment that raises the levels of catecholamines and serotonin in the brain will relieve depression. Exercise is one of the ways you can help to increase these brain chemicals. Take long walks or short vigorous walks; exhaust yourself with activity. Sunshine also turns on nature's serotonin production. Take advantage of every sunny day.

Eat a healthy diet. Include fresh fruits and vegetables in abundance in your menu planning, and don't forget the complex carbohydrates in pasta or the protein in lean chicken or turkey.

And finally, find ways to pamper yourself. Shop. Take long baths. Try a new hair color. Change your style. Surround yourself with flowers. Turn on some happy music.

Using traditional medicine.—Estrogen does increase the levels of catecholamines and serotonin, and it will stop the hot flashes often responsible for keeping you awake at night. While estrogen is not an antidepressive drug, many women find depression is lifted once hormone replacement therapy is begun.

Other possibilities.—While some depression is common during menopause, it could also be caused by other medical conditions, such as diabetes. Thus, it is important to discuss this symptom with your doctor. You will want to be tested to get to the bottom of whatever the chemical imbalance is that causes you to feel nonproductive.

Psychological therapy was shown in one study to be more effective than antidepressant drugs in alleviating severe depression. Even more interesting, reading about such therapy was found to be effective as well. The value of talking about your concerns cannot be underestimated, but a word of caution. *Don't hold yourself responsible for the state of the world.* It took a lot of us working at cross purposes to let things get this bad. Be assured that your perceptions are correct; the world is a pretty crazy place.

You are far from alone in your worries. Most people confront depression at some point in their lives. One researcher reported that the incidence of depression is no greater among menopausal women than any other population group. The greatest incidence, according to that study, is among young women (as with the post-partum blues). Men often experience depression as well.

DESIRE TO BE ALONE

Pat was one of the most gregarious women in town. She loved people and continually sought out the company of others. She was the perfect hostess and often entertained in her home. Once she rounded the corner on 50, however, she lost all interest in her friends and wanted only to be left alone. What's the problem?

During the years surrounding menopause, a host of emotional changes accompany the physical ones. The desire to be alone is a common psychological change. You may feel you need more time to think things through. Perhaps you're exhausted from sleepless nights. Maybe you are just tired of taking care of others. More likely, you need to come to terms with the many changes taking place in your life.

What can you do about needing isolation?

There's nothing wrong with wanting to be alone—for a while, anyway. If your desire for isolation lingers, however, depression could be the real problem.

Helping yourself.—Take time to be alone, but then force yourself to move out into the world again. Everyone needs time alone, so schedule some for yourself. Take naps, read books, rest, meditate, enjoy solitary activities. But don't allow yourself to become totally isolated. Recognize that there are healthy limits to both togetherness and solitude.

Using traditional medicine.—As with all the other signs of menopause, if there is some chemical element in this need for isolation, it probably revolves around activity in the hypothalamus or pituitary

---

Moments of Madness

•

SPOTTED ON A T SHIRT:

ASK ME ABOUT MY VOW OF SILENCE!

gland. Both of these glands are involved in your menstrual cycle. There is not much information available to explain why you might feel this way, but there is evidence that you are not alone in wanting to be alone.

Other possibilities.—One of the best things you can do when you want to be left alone is to try to seek out the company of your peers. Join a menopause support group or, if there isn't one in your area, start one. Get involved in an entirely new activity or exercise. Start a hobby that requires you to go get a little training. Work your way back into the world.

DIGESTIVE DISTRESSES

Marion sat in the bathroom. It seemed she had been there for hours, but nothing happened. She had always been quite regular, but once she turned 46, everything seemed to change. Now her biggest daily challenge was combatting what seemed like chronic constipation, yet her stomach was constantly churning with what felt like terrible gas pains.

Why do so many foods seem disagreeable?

Gastrointestinal upset is a common complaint of women during the years surrounding menopause. Constipation, diarrhea, and indigestion are frequent menopausal plights, along with a greatly increased production of intestinal gas.

Estrogen receptors in the stomach and small intestine are affected by the fluctuating levels of hormones. Less estrogen can mean more hydrochloric acid in the stomach, causing digestive discomfort. More progesterone causes the intestinal tract to slow down, so waste takes longer to work its way through the bowel. This can cause constipation and gas.

Your liver, too, can be affected during the menopausal years. The liver is essentially a recycling center. The hormones your

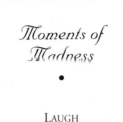

Moments of Madness

•

LAUGH
AND THE WORLD
LAUGHS WITH YOU.

PASS GAS
AND YOU SLEEP
ALONE.

body produces daily are broken down by the liver, and their components become available for the production of other hormones. Some hormones, such as LH and FSH, are produced in such enormous quantities that the liver becomes dedicated to this activity, and other digestive tasks are left undone.

On the other hand, gallbladder disease is also a problem for many women during these years. Be sure to consult your doctor if you are uncomfortable for any length of time.

What can you do about stomachaches?

If you are not on hormone replacement therapy, starting may ease some of the problems. If your digestive distress is related to hormone therapy, ask your doctor about other medications that can help. If you suspect gallstones, consult your doctor immediately.

Helping yourself.—Managing your diet is step one. A high-carbohydrate, low-fat diet seems to counteract a lot of digestive distress. White flour and meat products are known to slow the digestive process, so go for whole-grain foods, eat lots of vegetables, and drink lots of water. Bran causes problems for some women, so if you're trying a high-fiber diet for the first time, increase your fiber gradually. Also, don't overdo the bran. Some experts have suggested too much bran interferes with the uptake of calcium needed to keep bones strong and healthy. Instead try eating some prunes.

For minor digestive problems, drinking a cup of peppermint tea after a meal may be helpful, and ginger tea or even flat ginger ale can provide relief.

Try to eat at regular times, and use the toilet at regular times. Massaging the lower abdomen can sometimes start the action that promotes elimination.

Using traditional medicine.—Hormone replacement therapy seems to restore the normal gastrointestinal balance in many women. In the presence of gallstones, however, surgery may be needed. While the removal of a gallbladder was once a major procedure, that's no longer the case. In some locations, this surgery can be done as an outpatient procedure. Talk to your doctor. If surgery is indicated, ask about a laparoscopic chole-cystectomy—the so-called buttonhole operation.

Other possibilities.—If your gallbladder is not diseased, you should ask to be checked for ulcers, diverticulitis, or reflux. All of these conditions are associated with an increase in stomach acid. There are many medications available, both prescription and over-the-counter, to make you more comfortable.

DIZZINESS

Ruth stood at the top of the stairs. She grabbed the rail to start the trip down, but she was overcome by a sense of dizziness. She was afraid to take a step because she felt she would lose her balance. "What's happening to me?" she cried. Her friend came to her aid and led her back to the bedroom, but Ruth was totally shaken.

Dizziness can be related to changes occurring in the nervous system and in the blood vessels. The fine blood vessels that supply your nervous system contain estrogen receptors. A lack of estrogen to these receptors may lead to the dizzy feelings. This can be complicated even further by increases and decreases in other hormones.

The liver is also implicated in the process. It may be overtaxed by the excess of LH and FSH, two hormones that are produced in abundance during the menopausal years. Without estrogen to counteract the process, the liver must work harder to break down these substances. With liver function concentrated on this activity, other tasks usually performed may be left undone. Dizziness may be an indirect consequence.

Dizziness may also be caused by reduced blood flow to the brain, hyperventilation resulting from anxiety or fatigue, or inner ear disturbances.

What can you do to alleviate feelings of dizziness?

Once you understand the mechanisms responsible for the dizziness, you can begin to protect yourself from it.

Helping yourself.—Obvious things to do when you're feeling out of balance include lying down, waiting the dizziness out, and breathing deeply with your eyes closed. Recycle the air by breathing into your cupped hands. Exhale as slowly as possible. Sometimes concentrating on something completely separate from whatever you were doing can help. Smelling lavender oil is also said to relieve dizziness, similar to the bygone tradition of using smelling salts.

Using traditional medicine.—Because of its relationship to hormonal imbalance, this symptom can often be counteracted by hormone replacement therapy. Once the estrogen deficiency is corrected, the liver will return to its former activity, breaking down and recycling all the other body chemicals.

Other possibilities.—Alcohol and the use of certain prescription drugs can diminish the blood supply to the brain and make you dizzy. Be aware of the potential effects of all the prescription medications you take and abide by the instructions for their use. Minimize your use of alcohol during the years when the liver is already overtaxed.

Dry Eyes

June looked in the mirror. Her eyes looked bloodshot and felt dry and scratchy. She rubbed them to force some tears, but nothing worked. "What's wrong?" she thought. "I hope this isn't the beginning of serious eye disease."

As we get older, the lenses of the eyes, which are made of a gel-like material, begin to harden. As this occurs, vision often changes. Tired eyes and headaches also can be signs of this process. Around the time of menopause, mucous membranes become thinner and the tear glands don't work as well as they once did. Consequently, many women experience dry eyes.

What can you do to care for your eyes?

Protecting your vision is a life-long commitment. Regular vision screenings, glaucoma tests, and cataract inspections should be scheduled at least every two years once you reach age 35.

Helping yourself.—Artificial tears often can help keep your eyes moist. There are many products available over the counter, but it's a good idea to ask your doctor what's best for you.

Using traditional medicine.—If your dry eyes are related to hormonal changes, you should get some relief from hormone replacement therapy. Regular eye exams and changes in prescription lenses as needed also are important.

Glaucoma is one of the leading causes of blindness, affecting two of every 100 people over the age of 35. With glaucoma, pressure builds up inside the eye, endangering the optic nerve. By the time you notice your sight is changing, however, it may be too late to reverse the process. The test for glaucoma is simple and painless and could very well save your sight.

Other possibilities.—If you have diabetes, you are susceptible to a condition known as diabetic retinopathy, which causes leaking of blood vessels at the back of the eye. Lasers can be used to seal the leaking blood vessels in a painless procedure. Left untreated, the condition leads to blindness. Eye changes also can occur with rheumatoid arthritis. Unexplained redness should always be checked out with an ophthalmologist.

DRY MOUTH

Betty Lou felt like she could "spit cotton." She had heard her cowboy husband and his friends talk about how dry it was out on the prairie, but she never knew that feeling until lately. Something was changing and she found that she coughed frequently and her mouth felt dry.

Dry mouth is a recognized side effect of more than 400 different medications. It is also a normal part of the aging process. But the lowered estrogen levels associated with menopause seem to make the problem even worse. In addition to the discomfort of dry mouth, a lack of saliva can contribute to an increase in gum disease and cavities.

What can you do about that cotton-mouth feeling? In addition to good dental care, you'll want to do something to increase the saliva flow to keep your mouth moist. (Read the section on dental problems, page 53.)

Helping yourself.—You may want to try chewing sugar-free gum or sucking on sugarless drops to keep the saliva flowing. Drink lots of water, sipping frequently to keep your mouth moist.

Using traditional medicine.—Hormone replacement therapy helps many women who experience this drying phenomenon. While the actual science behind this disorder is not clear, most physicians agree it is a real problem for many women.

Other possibilities.—Antihistamines, antidepressants, and antihypertensives all contribute to the drying out of tissue. If you are taking any of these on a regular basis, dry mouth may be a side effect.

DRY SKIN

Genevieve itched. Her feet itched, her arms itched, the back of her hands itched. She looked into the mirror and the wrinkles in her face made her feel sad. "Oh, sure," she sighed, "I know I earned all of these in my 60 years, but I'm tired of wearing my badges every day. What's a woman to do?"

Because sebaceous glands in your skin produce less lubrication, dry skin is a common problem as we get older. But many menopausal women say they feel dry inside and out.

What can you do about keeping your skin moist and supple?

There are lots of ways to moisturize. Using lotions, eliminating drying soaps, and wearing cotton-lined rubber gloves when you wash dishes can all help. Use bath oils and don't bathe too frequently. Daily bathing can deplete skin of valuable moisture, so consider sponge baths instead of soaking baths. Use lukewarm, not hot, water for baths and showers. Hot water opens pores and promotes drying.

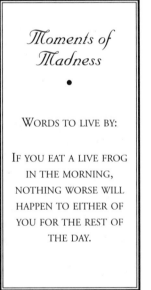

Moments of Madness

•

WORDS TO LIVE BY:

IF YOU EAT A LIVE FROG IN THE MORNING, NOTHING WORSE WILL HAPPEN TO EITHER OF YOU FOR THE REST OF THE DAY.

Helping yourself.—A healthy diet is your best defense against aging. Vitamins A, B, D, and E have all been proven to be good for the skin. Drinking plenty of water is another excellent defense from dryness.

Using lotions and creams can really help combat the discomfort and itching of dry skin. For your face, a moisturizing cream is better than a lotion. Read the labels and find one that is noncomedogenic so it doesn't clog your pores.

If you tend to have acne, don't use lotions or creams containing lanolin, heavy oils, or cocoa butter. When you moisturize your face in the morning, wait 15 to 20 minutes before you put your makeup on. This will give the cream a chance to penetrate the skin.

Using traditional medicine.—Much of the dryness you experience outside is also taking place inside your body. Hormone replacement therapy may alleviate the problem, but don't underestimate the role of environmental factors. Wind, cold temperatures, indoor heat, and low humidity play major roles as well. Lotions and creams can help restore the moisture to your skin.

Other possibilities.—In addition to faces and hands, feet will also require some extra attention for virtually any woman over age 40. You'll probably notice that your heels become dry and cracked. Try using a pumice stone to remove the dead skin. Then apply a thick moisturizing cream.

Your fingernails also need moisture, and they grow more slowly after about age 40. If you use polish, don't change it too often. Both the polish and the remover strip your nails of valuable moisture.

EMOTIONAL UPHEAVAL

(See Mood Swings)

ERRATIC MENSTRUATION

Julia had on her best white skirt. She thought she was ready to head out the door to the luncheon and book lecture at the women's club. Then she felt something warm and wet, and she headed to the bathroom. "Oh no," she cried in dismay, "Not again. I just had a period a week ago. What's going on? Am I sick? Do I have cancer or something?"

Sally hadn't had her period in eight months. She didn't think about it much, she just kind of assumed that because she was 52 years old she was finished. She thought menopause was highly overrated because she didn't really have any problems at all. Then she got another period. "After eight months," she sighed, "give me a break. I thought I was done with all that."

During your years of normal menstruation, the production of FSH from the pituitary gland and estrogen from the ovaries is in balance. Prolonged secretion of estrogen without ovulation, however, can make the ovaries resistant to FSH stimulation. The lining of the uterus becomes extra thick, and unusually large amounts of blood are shed during your period.

After ovulation, your ovaries produce progesterone, another player in this delicate cycle. When you do not ovulate, you don't produce progesterone, nor will your uterus shed its lining on a regular basis. Consequently, some women have heavy periods during the perimenopausal years while others have infrequent menstruation, possibly heavy, possibly not.

What can you do about irregular periods?

If you are having more than one period in a typical 30-day cycle, talk to your doctor. He or she will want to check to find out exactly what's going on.

It is not abnormal to have more frequent periods as you approach menopause, just as it is not abnormal to have your periods less often during these same years. As a matter of fact, most women notice changes in their periods during their 30s. The pattern continues to change throughout the 40s, and by the time women reach menopause, there seems to be no standard for what to expect.

There are many factors influencing production of estrogen besides the hypothalamic-pituitary-ovarian cycle described earlier. Body size, diet, and physical activity all contribute to the body's ability to respond to the changes occurring around menopause. Other external factors, such as stress, medication, and use of tranquilizers, can also affect menstrual cycles.

Helping yourself.—As you approach menopause, it's a good idea to keep track of your periods. You'll want to follow your own irregularities and be aware of signs of trouble. Any of the following can signal potential problems, although they are all considered normal in menopause:

- Heavy blood flow
- Longer than usual periods
- Increased frequency of periods
- Spotting between periods
- Cramping, particularly if you never had cramps before
- Bleeding after a period of 12 months with no bleeding

Other things you can do for yourself include:
- Avoid alcohol, which impedes the formation of blood platelets responsible for clotting
- Try taking an anti-inflammatory drug, such as Advil®, Nuprin® or Ponstel®
- Exercise regularly. Exercise lowers the production of FSH and LH and generally helps you feel better.

Using traditional medicine.—Seeing your gynecologist regularly during the menopausal years is vital in the effort to remain healthy. Progesterone therapy is usually prescribed for abnormal bleeding. A combination of estrogen and progesterone often corrects cyclic irregularities.

Other possibilities.—If you have very heavy periods for any length of time, you may want to have a blood test for anemia. Loss of large amounts of blood can lead to iron-deficiency, which affects the body's ability to carry oxygen.

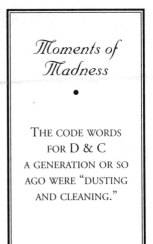

Moments of Madness

•

THE CODE WORDS
FOR D & C
A GENERATION OR SO
AGO WERE "DUSTING
AND CLEANING."

There are other conditions that can cause heavy vaginal bleeding, all of which will require medical attention. Don't assume that a heavier-than-usual period is totally normal if you feel extremely tired or if you have unusual discomfort. Get it checked out.

Other conditions associated with heavy bleeding include endometrial hyperplasia and cancer of the uterus. Also, fibroids, which are benign muscular growths of the uterine wall, can cause heavy bleeding. You'll want to know if you have any fibroids before you start hormone replacement therapy. Rapidly growing fibroids may require a hysterectomy, but only if there are significant symptoms, and only after other treatments have failed.

One possible treatment used for heavy or "dysfunctional" bleeding is called dilation and curettage (D & C). It is a minor surgical procedure in which the cervix is dilated (stretched) and the uterus is scraped and cleaned with an instrument called a curette. It is one of the most common procedures done in the United States, with about one in every 200 women having a D & C each year.

FATIGUE OR WEAKNESS

Sally sat at her typewriter. She felt as though she could doze off, even though she had a stack of envelopes to address. She sighed deeply. Her hands felt so heavy, the effort to put her fingers on the keys seemed to be exhausting. "How can this be? I slept nine hours last night, and I had at least eight the night before." She was puzzled. "Why am I so tired all the time?"

Fatigue is one of the most common complaints heard during the perimenopausal years. Usually it is a result of the reduced estrogen levels that contribute to sleeplessness and irritability, but it can also be caused by changes in testosterone levels.

Testosterone, sometimes referred to as the "male hormone," makes you feel energetic and triggers your sex drive. If you have no interest in sex and you feel tired all the time, chances are your testosterone levels are falling.

As was mentioned earlier, insomnia is a common cause of fatigue and can be related to hormone levels. It's not unusual for women to wake up repeatedly during the night because they need to urinate or because of a hot flash or sweating. Some women wake up for no reason and then worry the night away—an exhausting experience in itself.

Regardless of what causes the sleep deprivation, a feeling of chronic fatigue is the result.

What can you do to feel more energized?

Helping yourself.—A good place to start might be to change your diet. Eliminate caffeine if you can, and stay away from alcohol before bedtime. Eat lightly in the evening. Drink a glass of warm milk at bedtime, or try taking a relaxing bath. Use meditation or relaxation techniques to help yourself get back to sleep once you've been awake.

Prioritize your activities, and manage your energy as efficiently as you can. Take time to rest during the day (napping is known to increase life span). Daily exercise, even when you don't feel like it, is one of the best ways to add zest to your life (not to mention the many other benefits). Try to maintain a positive attitude. Even if you are tired, try pretending you're not. You might be surprised at the result.

Using traditional medicine.—If your fatigue is related to hormonal changes, you should begin to feel more energized once you starting using hormone therapy. If your fatigue is not related to hormone deficiency, you'll want your doctor to help you uncover the cause and figure out what to do.

Chronic fatigue syndrome (CFS) is now recognized as a legitimate medical problem. However, it can be difficult to diagnose. This condition is associated with severe fatigue that lasts at least six months. The following symptoms are considered part of the chronic fatigue syndrome:

- Chills or mild fever
- Swollen or painful lymph glands
- Muscle discomfort
- Sore throat
- Mysterious or unexplained muscle weakness
- Headache
- Joint pain
- Forgetfulness, irritability, confusion, depression, inability to concentrate
- Disturbed sleep

Many of these same symptoms also are common during perimenopausal years, which contributes to the difficult diagnosis. CFS, however, is thought to be caused by a virus or several viruses. In many cases, the fatigue is preceded by some infection or the flu.

At this time, there is no known cure for CFS. Treatments vary from mild antidepressant use to immune-system boosters. Antiviral agents, gamma globulin, vitamin B_{12} shots, and histamine blockers are among possible treatments, but check with a health care professional if you think you have this problem.

Other possibilities.—Fatigue can also result from nutritional deficiency, so be sure to get all the nutrients you need by eating sensibly. Tiredness also is a symptom of iron-deficiency anemia and thyroid disease. Many diseases can cause fatigue, so if hormone replacement therapy doesn't help you, talk to your doctor about what else might be going on.

FEAR OF BEING ALONE IN PUBLIC

(See also Anxiety)

Janet felt rushed. She had to get to the mall to finish her Christmas shopping. All of a sudden she felt as though she simply couldn't go. The fear she felt of being alone in the mall overwhelmed her. She felt desperately afraid of losing control. "I'm going crazy," she thought. "I have all this shopping to do and I'm completely paralyzed by this irrational fear. I even know it's irrational. Right after the holidays I'm going to find a good psychiatrist."

Where does this fear come from?

Your adrenal glands are responsible for the "fight or flight" response characterized by increased adrenaline levels in times of heightened stress.

During the menopausal years, the adrenals work double time to try to maintain hormonal balance. The overworked adrenals seem to overreact, sensing that even the most minor situations are crises. This gives rise to the sensations of anxiety, fear, and nervousness.

What can you do about feeling afraid?

Sometimes the fear of being alone in public places has a psychological component as well. You may feel as though something is about to happen, something disastrous, and you know that you can't cope with it on your own. You may also simply feel a need for increased support during the years surrounding menopause when you are experiencing so much change in your body.

Helping yourself.—Janet was on the right track by recognizing that her fear was not necessarily rational. But that didn't make the feeling go away. Sometimes just the knowledge that this symptom is recognized as one of the primary symptoms of menopause can be helpful. Knowing this can reduce the amount of stress you place on yourself for feeling something that you think you shouldn't feel.

Remember that fear arises when we feel unsafe. Find out what you need to do to feel safe. Get support from your mate or your friends. Discuss the feeling. Try using mental imagery to create a safe space for yourself in your mind. When you feel this fear rising in you, take slow deep breaths and put yourself into the picture of the safe space you've created for yourself.

Using traditional medicine.—Like the other classical symptoms of menopause, fear of being alone in a public place often disappears once hormone replacement therapy is begun. If that doesn't work or isn't an option for you, you might want to talk to a counselor, especially if your fear is keeping you at home.

Other possibilities.—If your fear is based on feelings of vulnerability, you might consider taking a class in self-defense. Yoga exercises also can be helpful.

FIBROIDS

Sylvia was really frightened. Something was wrong. Her period, a very heavy one, had already lasted seven days. The pain in her lower back was almost as troublesome as the pressure she felt in her lower abdomen. She resolved to call her gynecologist that day.

What are uterine fibroids and where do they come from?

About 20 percent of women over the age of 35 develop what are known as uterine fibroids. These are also called leiomyomas, myomas, or fibromyomas.

These are normally harmless growths that develop in or on the muscular wall of the uterus. Estrogen has been implicated in their growth, since women on birth control pills or hormone replacement therapy seem more prone to develop fast-growing fibroids than women not taking hormones.

Because fibroids are generally slow growing, most of them cause no symptoms or discomfort. But they can be troublesome if they become large. If a fibroid grows large enough, it can press against the bladder and bowel and cause stress incontinence or constipation. Fibroids can also cause pelvic pain, heavy bleeding, and infertility.

What can you do about fibroids?

Helping yourself.—A yearly exam by your gynecologist is a good place to start. Usually the doctor can detect any fibroids during this routine check. If they are not causing any trouble, you'll just work with your doctor to keep tabs on their growth. If you are approaching menopause and have decided against hormone replacement therapy, the fibroids will usually shrink and disappear at this time.

Using traditional medicine.—Surgical treatment includes removal of small fibroids by hysteroscopy, D & C (dilation and curettage), or via a procedure known as myomectomy. In myomectomy, a surgeon removes the fibroids from the uterus, then repairs the tissue to preserve the womb.

Other possibilities.—Fibroids reappear in about 10 percent of women who have had myomectomies. If some fibroids have already been removed but others return, removal of the uterus may be considered. Hysterectomy is the procedure recommended. Ask your doctor about preserving your ovaries to spare you from the effects of "sudden menopause." (See Chapter 4 for complete information.)

FLUSHING

(See also Hot Flashes)

Liz was at school, teaching her fourth graders a unit in science, when she felt a rush of heat rising from her chest to her neck and up to the top of her head. Her face turned red, and she began to perspire. "Excuse me, class," she announced. "We'll continue this lesson in a moment. I'll be right back."

She left the room in a panic, thinking she had just contracted a case of the flu or that her blood pressure was out of control. She raced into the teacher's lounge. "I must be sick," she said to her colleague, Annette. "I'm running a temperature, and I feel as though my face is on fire." Annette smiled and said, "Welcome to the Fan Club. What you're feeling is the flushing that goes with a hot flash. It's nothing serious, but I've had them and I know how uncomfortable they can be."

What is flushing?

Flushing is the "power surge" related to hot flashes, which occur because of disturbances in the body's temperature regulation. Flushing is the rush of blood, usually in the face and neck, that comes with a hot flash.

Not all women experience this reddening, but those who do report being a bit embarrassed by this telltale sign of midlife. Some women redden uniformly up their necks and faces; others have red blotches scattered over the area.

What can you do about flushing?

Helping yourself.—As with hot flashes, take action to cool yourself down. Wear layered clothing, fan yourself, keep some ice water handy, and use cool damp cloths on your brow when you need them.

Using traditional medicine.—As is true of most of the symptoms of menopause, flushing generally disappears with hormone replacement therapy. The flushing that comes with hot flashes seems to be related to the withdrawal of the hormone estrogen, which destabilizes the temperature regulation functions of the hypothalamus and causes abnormal releases of pituitary hormones. Once the levels of estrogen in your body are restored, flushing seems to disappear.

Other possibilities.—There is the outside possibility that the flushing you are experiencing is related to another illness. High blood pressure, thyroid disease, and a number of other disorders can all cause reddening of the skin and night sweating. All these conditions may need to be ruled out at the start and certainly deserve your doctor's attention if hormone replacement therapy has not eliminated symptoms after four to six weeks.

FOOT AND LEG CRAMPS

(See Aching Joints and Muscles and
Cramps in the Legs and Feet)

FORMICATION (ITCHING, CRAWLING SKIN)

Sue felt as though she was covered with fire ants. Her skin was itching, and she felt as though the ants were crawling all over her body. She was so sensitive that she couldn't bear to even touch her own hands. "I've read about this," she thought. "This happens to people who are having DTs or quitting drugs. But I don't do drugs. This must be all in my head. I'm really going crazy."

What causes the feeling of bugs crawling over your skin?

The technical name for this buggy sensation is "formication." What's happening is that the nerve endings in the skin are extremely sensitive. While experts attribute this variously to the hypothalamus and to the liver, most agree that about 10 percent of American women do experience this at some time during the perimenopausal years.

What can you do about it?

Helping yourself.—If you should experience this sensation of bugs crawling over your body, don't panic! Talk to someone about it. Do what you need to do to get comfortable. Usually this lasts only a few moments, but they are uncomfortable moments. Remove irritating clothing until the attack passes.

Using traditional medicine.—Discuss this with your doctor, but don't expect any clear explanations for this weird feeling. No one really knows exactly what's going on. It usually resolves after a few weeks. Hormones help some women.

Other possibilities.—The Chinese have used food cures for centuries. One such remedy is to eat raw beets, grated or

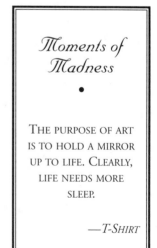

Moments of Madness

•

THE PURPOSE OF ART IS TO HOLD A MIRROR UP TO LIFE. CLEARLY, LIFE NEEDS MORE SLEEP.

—*T-Shirt*

juiced, three times in one day. We have no idea how this relieves the itching, crawling symptoms, but it seems worth a try if you are really uncomfortable. (These Chinese traditions have been around for 5,000 years, so there just may be something to them.)

FREQUENT URINATION OR LOSS OF URINARY CONTROL

(See Loss of Urinary Control)

 ## GASTRIC UPSET AND GALLBLADDER DISEASE

(See also Digestive Distresses)

Betty Ann started hormone replacement therapy when she was 34, after her total abdominal hysterectomy. Now at 54, she is having mysterious pains that radiate to her back. She checked with her doctor and learned the problem is gallbladder disease. Isolated stones are causing the pain. She has decided to have a laparoscopic cholecystectomy.

Who gets gallbladder disease?

A major research project, the Nurses' Health Study, has provided evidence linking estrogen replacement therapy to an increase in gallbladder disease. The study followed 55,000 postmenopausal women for eight years. The results showed that estrogen users were twice as likely to have gallstones requiring removal as were women who had never taken hormones.

The study did not, however, consider two factors that might have altered the

---

Moments of Madness

•

NEVER DRINK COFFEE AT LUNCH. IT WILL KEEP YOU AWAKE ALL AFTERNOON.

results. It did not examine the rate of less serious gallbladder disease among the two populations, nor did it look at whether those women who took estrogen were more likely to see their doctors more frequently and therefore be treated for gallbladder disease than the other women.

What can you do about gallbladder disease?

Helping yourself.—The amount of fat in your diet and your weight are even more important than hormones in determining whether you are likely to get gallbladder disease.

Using traditional medicine.—Be sure to discuss any history of gallbladder disease with your doctor when you talk about hormone replacement therapy. The benefits of hormone therapy are important for many women, and today, laparoscopic removal of the gallbladder is relatively safe and easy.

GRIEF

(See also Depression)

Amy sat and cried. She didn't really know why. She only knew she felt miserable and lonely. She wasn't just sad, she was in mourning. But no one had died. "I'm absolutely crazy," she thought. "I know I need to see a psychiatrist, but when I'm asked what's wrong, I can't answer."

Why do you feel like you've just lost your best friend?

The feelings of loss many women have during the perimenopausal years seems to be almost universal—and very unpleasant. Some doctors (probably men) have suggested that women miss their periods. (It sure would be fun to read your minds right now!)

What is much more likely to be the case is that during midlife women do begin to experience more losses. Some lose jobs, some lose careers, most lose their parents. The kids move away, and the pets have to be put to sleep. Who wouldn't be grieving?

What can you do about feelings of loss?

Helping yourself.—If you need to grieve, grieve. Get it out of your system. Grief is one of those emotional states that must be expressed. Repressed grief can cause great psychological damage. If you need help in learning to express your grief, see a psychologist or read about the grief of others and cry for them.

One of the great classics on the subject is *A Grief Observed,* by C.S. Lewis, also in a movie version entitled *Shadowland.* This tragic and hopeful passage of a man who lost the great love of his life to cancer takes us from the moment of terrible loss to his adjustment to life without her. It will bring tears to your eyes, but it will also gently guide you through the stages of grief.

For a more definitive study of the grieving process, read *On Death and Dying,* by Elisabeth Kubler-Ross. She explains the stages of grief, starting with the first days of denial and ending with the reconciliation of life in a new perspective. These works are considered classics in the field and should be helpful in understanding what you are going through.

Using traditional medicine.—Some of the emotional ups and downs of menopause can be ameliorated by hormone therapy, but many must be lived through. Talk to your doctor if your grief feels never ending or hopeless.

Other possibilities.—It is not clear whether large doses of vitamin B complex, the so-called "stress" vitamin, relieve the emotional stress of grief, but some reports show depression gets better when these vitamins are taken.

HAIR GROWTH

$\mathcal{H}$

(See Increased Hair Growth)

HAIR LOSS

Joanna looked in the mirror. The top of her head was showing through her hair. She felt panicky. "What's happening to me?" she cried in despair. "I'm going bald. I must have cancer or some other horrible disease. What can I do?"

Some hair loss at midlife is perfectly natural. What's happening is that the tissue surrounding hair follicles (the place where each individual hair has a root) is made up mostly of collagen. The follicle root is deep inside the skin. When moisture is withdrawn from the collagen, the hair loses its support and falls out.

What can you do about thinning hair and receding hairline?

Helping yourself.—If your hair loss is really troublesome, be sure to talk with your doctor. There are some serious health conditions that involve such hair loss. If you have what we call "normal" hair loss, with some shedding of hair in your comb or hairbrush, some evidence of hair on your pillowcase, or hair on the shower stall floor after shampooing, you don't need to be concerned. Most people lose 50 to 75 hairs every day. After shampooing, we lose about 250.

Using traditional medicine.—Serious hair loss with bald patches on your scalp warrants medical attention. For women, hormonal imbalances can cause this loss. Sometimes an excess of the male hormone testosterone causes a deepening of the voice along with hair loss. Getting the hormones back in balance usually fixes this, and hair regrows in about six months.

There is a topical form of the blood-pressure medication minoxidil (Rogaine®), that seems to stimulate hair growth in both men and women. If you are really bothered by hair loss, this could be an option to consider.

Other possibilities.—Sometimes hair loss occurs because the hair shaft is weak and breaks off easily. The use of too many chemicals on the hair is usually at the root of this problem (pun intended, of course). Treat your hair gently, and be careful with hot hair dryers and curling irons. Using a cream rinse or a protein conditioner after shampooing helps reduce friction and strengthens individual hair fibers.

HEADACHES AND MIGRAINES

Donna knew a headache was coming on. She had seen the aura and felt the wave of nausea that warned her what was ahead. It had been happening to her for some years now, and she knew she had to get home and get to bed. When the full pain of the headache hit, it was blinding and made her feel sick to her stomach. "I have to get help," she said. "Can't somebody do something about these terrible headaches?"

For many women, migraine headaches occur more often during the perimenopause. Again, we don't know exactly why. On the other hand, headaches linked with menstruation or ovulation often disappear at menopause. These headaches are believed to be triggered by fluctuations in hormone levels, and once these levels even out, the problem disappears.

What can you do about headaches?

Helping yourself.—Headaches sometimes are a signal that your body needs to take it easy. The perimenopausal years can be stressful for your body. You may need more rest and relaxation. Aspirin and other painkillers can give you immediate relief, but habitual use of any substance sometimes make the problem worse instead of better.

Be aware of your body. Migraine pain is caused by extracerebral vasodilation (meaning something that causes the veins in your head to open up). Sometimes such headaches are triggered by food allergies. Among the foods implicated in migraine headaches are citrus fruit, yogurt, aged cheeses, red wine, chocolate, and tomatoes. Monosodium glutamate (MSG), commonly found in Chinese food, and nitrates also cause problems for many people.

Using traditional medicine.—Hormone replacement therapy improves the picture for many migraine sufferers. Estrogen raises the level of natural pain-relievers in the brain and stabilizes mood-altering substances produced there (dopamine and serotonin). This probably explains why estrogen often eliminates migraine headaches altogether.

On the other hand, progesterone (the other player in hormone replacement therapy) may cause a recurrence of headaches and mood swings. This is something you must work out with your doctor. By changing dosages and hormone types, the problem often can be eliminated.

When headaches worsen instead of improve with hormone replacement therapy, you may need to consider other treatments. Among them are the nonsteroidal anti-inflammatory drugs (NSAIDs), such as Disalcid. Inderal, propranolol, and timolol beta-adrenergic blockers also are options. Naproxen sodium is useful for premenstrual headaches.

For acute migraines, dihydro-ergotamine (DHE), injected intramuscularly, has proved very effective. There is a new alternative to this, Imitrex, but the cost is significantly higher and there is no evidence that this drug, also taken by injection, is any more effective than DHE. Finally, a vasoconstrictor, Sumatriptan, can counteract the mechanisms of migraine. All of these approaches should be discussed with your physician. All require a prescription.

Other possibilities.—Women who suffer menopausal migraines usually have a long history of migraines, and the cause may be hard to determine. If you suspect food allergies, avoid alcohol, red wines, cheeses, chocolate, peanuts, MSG, and other food-allergy sources. If you have debilitating headaches, a complete physical examination can help rule out other possible causes.

Migraines that develop after menopause are not always hormone related. To better understand what's going on, try keeping a migraine diary, noting the occurrence and severity of each attack, as well as any foods, beverages, weather conditions, stress, or sleep disturbances that might be related to the episode. Stress headaches often can be distinguished from true migraines by using a diary.

Other possible causes of headaches include visual problems, light sensitivity, pituitary tumors, or thyroid conditions, among others.

HEART PALPITATIONS

Betty was lying in bed, trying to sleep. Suddenly she felt a flutter in her chest. Then her heart began to pound. Her ears were ringing, and her face felt hot. "Oh, my God," she thought, "I'm having a heart attack." She tried to calm herself, and her heart began to slow down. She felt extremely frightened.

Heart palpitations, or pounding, racing heartbeats, are sometimes accompanied by hot flashes (or vice versa) during the perimenopausal years. While science has yet to explain exactly what's going on, some experts suspect the abnormal heartbeats are caused by electrolyte imbalances following profuse sweating. Whatever the cause, palpitations are recognized as a fairly common vasomotor disturbance related to menopause.

What can you do about palpitations?

Helping yourself.—Meditation is an excellent immediate first step in calming your racing heart. Place your hand on your heart, close your eyes, and breathe slowly, telling yourself to be calm.

Using traditional medicine.—Just as hot flashes often disappear with hormone replacement therapy, so do heart palpitations. There is some evidence that even women who have heart conditions, such as coronary artery disease or atherosclerotic heart disease, can benefit from hormone replacement.

Other possibilities.—It is possible that something serious is going on if your heart palpitations occur frequently. A complete cardiac workup is important for discovering what's going on. You can never be too responsive to these symptoms. When in doubt, call your doctor or 911.

HEAVY BLEEDING

For some women, the hormonal imbalances occurring once the ovaries begin to slow down result in excess estrogen and too little or no progesterone. Without progesterone, estrogen can cause excessive bleeding with clotting. One doctor told us to think of the progesterone as your period's "off" switch.

What can you do?

Helping yourself.—The biggest concern with this kind of bleeding is that it might also be caused by something much more serious than hormonal imbalance. No matter what the cause, heavy bleeding must be reported to your doctor. If everything is "normal" and you want to exercise some control over heavy bleeding at home, here are some tips suggested by other women:

- Avoid drinking alcoholic beverages. Alcohol may inhibit formation of blood platelets needed to form clots.
- Avoid taking hot showers or baths on days of heavy blood flow. Heat may increase bleeding because it causes blood vessels to open wider.
- Avoid aspirin. This is another platelet inhibitor
- Increase exercise. Strenuous exercise lowers production of FSH and LH which leads to lower levels of estrogen.
- Do get checked for signs of anemia. Talk to your doctor about your possible need for iron.
- Ask your doctor to check levels of FSH and LH, as well as thyroid functions.

Using traditional medicine.—If the bleeding is caused by an imbalance, hormone replacement may be the solution. If the bleeding is a sign of another condition, you'll want to know what it is. Possible causes include fibroids, polyps, nonmalignant tumors, or malignancy in the reproductive organs.

Other possibilities.—Your doctor might suggest a pelvic sonogram, an office endometrial sampling, or a D & C (dilation and curettage) to find out the cause. At times, an endometrial ablation or a hysterectomy may be necessary, depending on what's going on. Chapter 4 gives more information about these procedures.

HIGH CHOLESTEROL

Rachel had never had high cholesterol until she saw her doctor about three years after her menopause. Suddenly her levels were well above 300 when they were supposed to be below 200. "I don't know what's going on," she told her doctor. "I eat a low-fat diet, I exercise, and I never touch an egg."

Why do some women suddenly have high cholesterol levels after menopause?

Again, the answer isn't clear. But many experts believe cholesterol goes up because estrogen plays a role in liver functions and in the metabolism of cholesterol and other fats.

Estrogen is known to lower blood cholesterol, and it is also believed to increase receptors in the body that inactivate the bad cholesterol (LDL) and prevent it from turning into plaque. Researchers also have evidence that estrogen improves the usefulness of good cholesterol (HDL) by reducing the amount of the enzyme that destroys it. Estrogen deficiency increases the risk for cardiovascular disease. Hormone replacement therapy seems to protect the cardiovascular system in general.

What can you do about high cholesterol?

Helping yourself.—The number one approach to controlling high cholesterol is, of course, managing your diet. A diet low in saturated fats and cholesterol and high in fruits, vegetables, and whole grains is your best bet.

In addition to diet, exercise helps lower cholesterol levels. Regular aerobic (that is heart-strengthening) exercise for a minimum of 20 minutes daily or 60 minutes three times a week will strengthen your heart and raise your HDL level.

Using traditional medicine.—Because of the effects cited above, hormone replacement therapy should be considered if you are trying to combat high cholesterol. The full impact of various hormones on cholesterol, lipoproteins, and cardiovascular health is currently being investigated.

Other possibilities.—High fiber foods help lower cholesterol levels, so eat plenty of cereals, raw fruits and vegetables (with skins), and legumes (beans and peas).

HOT FLASHES

Moments of Madness

•

DON'T THINK
OF IT AS A HOT FLASH.
IT'S REALLY A
POWER SURGE.
AND WE'RE ALL POWER
SURGEONS LOOKING
FOR THE IDEAL SURGE
PROTECTOR!

(See also Flushing and Heart Palpitations)

It was a beautiful wintry day. Marion and some friends were heading for her lake cabin to go snowmobiling. The temperature outside was a balmy 12 degrees. But Marion felt like she was in the tropics. She feared her rising body temperature would make the windows in the car steam over.

Her friends noticed she was perspiring and said, "Hey, let's stop and roll around in the snow." "That's exactly how I feel right now," Marion sighed. "These hot flashes, are so overwhelming. I really can't believe this is normal."

Why so hot?

Hot flashes are the single most often reported symptom of menopause. About 85 percent of women have them at one time or another. The good news is they are not all severe and they are seldom incapacitating.

Hot flashes are one of the vasomotor symptoms of the perimenopause. While their cause isn't totally clear, researchers do know that hot flashes occur when your body's temperature control system goes out of whack. The brain then sends out the signal to open the blood vessels full bore, and you feel instant surges of heat and perspiration.

Hot flashes are sometimes accompanied by a flush or reddening of the skin of the neck and face. They are also often followed by chills, indicating the body succeeded in cooling itself down to the point where it needs to be warmed up again. Shivering is your body's way of warming itself.

What can you do about hot flashes?

Helping yourself.—There's no question about it, hot flashes are a pain! But you can prepare for them by dressing in layers, wearing natural fibers that breathe, and carrying something to fan yourself. (Friends of ours formed a "Fan Club" for perimenopausal women who want to share experiences.)

Exercise also is known to help hot flashers. Estrogen levels seem to increase with strenuous exercise, according to one study. Managing your diet by avoiding alcohol, coffee, chocolate, and spicy foods may also be helpful.

Using traditional medicine.—Hormone replacement therapy is the best known remedy for the power surge.

Other possibilities.—For women who are unable to use hormone replacement therapy, there are some alternatives based on dietary supplements. One of these, used for centuries in China, is dong quai. Considered useful for every gynecological ailment, dong quai is reported to help tone and "feed" the reproductive organs and thus it eases the hormonal transition. It is available at health food stores.

Ginseng, another natural herb, is considered by some herbalists to be a woman's greatest ally during menopause. It is reputed to maintain hormonal balance, and alleviate hot flashes. Drinking lots of ice water and taking vitamin E supplements also help some women.

Other preparations available for women unable to take hormones are Clonidine® and Bellergal S® (available only by prescription), Rejuvex® (an over-the-counter dietary supplement), and Femtrol® (a phytoestrogen-based over-the-counter dietary supplement).

Check these options out with your doctor or with the new Office of Alternative Medicine at the National Institutes of Health in Washington, D.C. You might also try using meditation and visualization to imagine that you feel cool.

HYPERTENSION (HIGH BLOOD PRESSURE)

Mary's blood pressure was normal for her entire life. Her weight was just about perfect, and her health, in general, was good to excellent. All of the sudden, her doctor noticed a change from normal blood pressure readings to consistently higher than healthy readings.

High blood pressure is often associated with an increase in low-density lipoprotein (LDL), the dangerous type of fat that is deposited as plaque on the walls of the blood vessels. This condition is referred to as atherosclerosis.

When an artery becomes clogged with fat, the blood pressure usually goes up and the heart pumps harder and harder to overcome the resistance. Eventually arteries may become so narrow that blood can't pass through at all. When blood flow is totally or partially blocked, a part of the brain or heart suffers some damage. This can result in a stroke or a heart attack.

What can you do about high blood pressure?

Helping yourself.—High blood pressure can be very serious and requires medical attention. An important first step in bringing blood pressure down is to control your diet. Cutting back on fat and reducing the sodium in your diet can help.

Exercise is another step you can take. Choose an exercise that burns calories and gets your heart pumping to strengthen the heart muscle. If you are already on medication for high blood pressure, ask your doctor about how you can help yourself lower your blood pressure.

Using traditional medicine.—Estrogen helps to maintain a healthy balance between LDL and HDL cholesterol levels during most of a woman's life. Several studies have shown that when estrogen is withdrawn, LDL levels increase dramatically. When women are on hormone replacement therapy, however, both their cholesterol levels and their risk for cardiovascular disease decrease.

Your doctor may want you to take blood pressure medications. Among them are the ACE (angiotensin converting enzyme) inhibitors or calcium channel blockers, alone or in combination.

Angiotensin is the most powerful vasoconstrictor in the human body. ACE inhibitors block its action, resulting in less tension in the blood vessels and lower blood pressure. Calcium channel blockers also relax the walls of blood vessels, and reduce blood pressure.

Other drugs often prescribed for hypertension include diuretics and beta blockers. Diuretics decrease blood volume by removing excess water. However, they can also wash out potassium, so if you take diuretics, be sure to get plenty of potassium in your diet. (Bananas are an excellent source.) Beta blockers are drugs that block the nerve signals that constrict the arteries. Talk to your doctor or pharmacist about how to use these drugs carefully.

Other possibilities.—Cutting back on consumption of red meat, coffee, table salt, and alcohol can have a beneficial effect on blood pressure. (Interestingly, vegetarians rarely have high blood pressure.) Some recent scientific studies suggest that garlic can help in some cases, but we need more information.

Also, deep relaxation and yoga breathing seem to calm the sympathetic nervous system, which in turn relaxes the small arteries and lowers the blood pressure.

INCONTINENCE

(See Loss of Urinary Control)

INCREASED HAIR GROWTH

Gretchen frowned at her reflection in the mirror. She was really depressed. It looked to her like she was growing a beard. There were coarse, dark hairs growing randomly across her chin, and she didn't like it. "Seems like I turned 50 and the bottom fell out of my world," she said to the mirror. "I'm losing the hair off my head and growing it on my face. Give me a break!"

Why does hair grow where it shouldn't and not where it should? Unfortunately, the increase in facial hair is another one of those signs that tells you you're heading into menopause. When estrogen production slows, testosterone, one of the male hormones women need for energy and sexual arousal, can jump into overdrive. Testosterone promotes growth of facial and body hair.

What can you do about excess facial and body hair?

Helping yourself.—Many women enlist the aid of a hypertrichologist, a hair specialist who uses electrolysis to permanently remove that unwanted hair. Depending on your tolerance to the tiny stings each electrical shock imposes, you can plan on spending about 45 minutes a week on this process. Judge how much hair is gone after one session and plan to spend up to a year to get the problem solved.

Using traditional medicine.—A medication called spironolactone (Aldactone®) inhibits unwanted hair growth in some cases. It blocks the testosterone receptors on the hair follicles on the face, chest, and abdomen, but not the head, pubic area, or underarms. This is something to discuss with your doctor and should be considered only if your problem is severe. Aldactone takes about eight months to show results.

Other possibilities.—Testosterone is produced in the adrenal glands, and sudden increased production may signal other serious problems. Rarely, tumors of the adrenal glands may be suspected. Cushing's syndrome, a condition in which the adrenal glands produce high amounts of cortisol, could also explain the hair growth.

Women with polycystic ovarian disease, which causes numerous small cysts within the ovaries, and those with other ovarian tumors may also have elevated testosterone levels. If you believe your hair growth is extremely abnormal, check with a professional.

INCREASED SEXUAL DESIRE

Lorraine had always enjoyed sex, and she had never been shy. But when she turned 48, she found herself thinking about sex more and more. In fact, she was obsessed with it. She found herself worrying about what was going on in her head. "Is there such a thing as a middle-aged nymphomaniac?" she brooded. "Am I off the deep end here?"

More often than not, sexual interest increases because the kids are out of the house or the fear of pregnancy is gone. However, some experts believe testosterone levels, which are responsible for sexual feelings, increase when estrogen production falls. Women who are given testosterone as part of hormone replacement therapy often report increased sexual desire and more frequent sexual fantasies. The conclusion for now seems to be if there is a link between a heightened sex drive and menopause, it may be both biological and psychological.

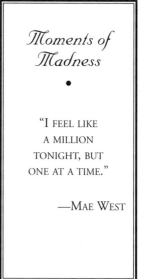

Moments of Madness

•

"I FEEL LIKE A MILLION TONIGHT, BUT ONE AT A TIME."

—MAE WEST

What can you do about a heightened sex drive?

Helping yourself.—There's nothing weird or unusual about feeling more sexy at this time in your life. In fact, you may want to consider "going with the feelings," since sex burns calories and keeps those muscles and tissues healthy. If you really are bothered, however, good aerobic exercise can burn up some of your excess energy.

Using traditional medicine.—If you believe your interest in sex is seriously out of balance, discuss it with your doctor. Treatment with a combination of estrogen, progesterone, and androgen usually restores equilibrium in these situations.

INSOMNIA (AND SLEEP DISTURBANCES)

Jane was awake again. For the third night in a row she couldn't sleep, and she wandered restlessly around her house. She turned on the TV, then surfed the channels to discover there was nothing of interest to her. She went to the kitchen and opened the refrigerator. Nothing interested her there. She went back to bed to toss and turn and finally, in frustration, got up and began her wanderings anew.

At midlife, women seem to be plagued by insomnia. Night sweats are often implicated in menopausal insomnia. Women who are awakened by feeling overheated and uncomfortable often have trouble getting back to sleep.

What can you do about wakefulness?

One or two sleepless nights don't make you an insomniac. There are some classic symptoms. If you awaken at night and find yourself still awake after 10 minutes, and this happens night after night, you probably really have insomnia. Likewise, if it takes you more than 30 minutes to fall asleep when you first go to bed, you've got insomnia. Finally, if you are taking a sleeping aid and you need it more than once or twice a week, you'll want to talk to your doctor about your sleeplessness.

Helping yourself.—High calcium foods or calcium supplements taken at bedtime help some women whose sleep problems are related to menopause. The proverbial glass of warm milk at bedtime can also promote sleep. Milk contains tryptophan, an amino acid that is believed to induce sleep.

Moments of Madness

•

INSOMNIA: TRIUMPH OF MIND OVER MATTRESS.

Using traditional medicine.—Normal sleep patterns return once hormone replacement therapy is stabilized for many women. If that isn't an option, however, there are some sleeping medications your doctor can prescribe if your sleeplessness is interfering with your life.

Other possibilities.—For the adventurous health-food connoisseur, foods such as kelp and hijiki, a mild-flavored seaweed, are said to help cure sleeping disorders. Also, there is recent evidence that melatonin tablets are highly effective with no serious side effects. Melatonin is the substance the brain normally produces to induce sleep.

IRRITABILITY

(See Mood Swings)

ITCHING

(See Formication and Vaginal dryness and itching)

LACK OF SEXUAL DESIRE

(See Decreased Sexual Desire)

LOSS OF URINARY CONTROL (INCONTINENCE)

(See also Bladder Changes and Infections)

It seemed to Sally that every time she sneezed she leaked a little urine. Now she was noticing that when she laughed, coughed, or even lifted something light, the problem was getting worse. She thought this was extreme, especially since she was only 49. "I must have a really serious disorder," she thought. "This just can't be normal."

Around the time of menopause, the muscles and tissues in the pelvic area become weak and stretched as a result of the drop in estrogen levels. Low estrogen levels may also decrease collagen in connective tissues and ligaments that support the urethra and reduce blood flow responsible for some of the pressure on the urethra.

All this means that slight stress incontinence may be predictable during menopause, but it does not have to be inevitable. Nonetheless, other reversible causes of urinary incontinence, such as bladder infections and fecal impaction, as well as side effect of some antidepressants and antihypertensive drugs, need to be ruled out.

In addition to stress urinary incontinence, such as Sally was experiencing, there are other forms of incontinence. These include overflow incontinence, where the bladder simply cannot handle the high demand placed on it, and urge incontinence, in which the need to urinate is so urgent, it becomes challenging or impossible to get to the bathroom quickly enough.

What can you do about urinary incontinence?

Helping yourself.—Kegel exercises are very effective for improving problems with incontinence. These are simple muscle tensing-relaxing movements that strengthen the pelvic floor muscles.

To do the Kegel exercises, first become aware of the muscles you use to start and stop your urinary flow. These are the muscles you need to strengthen. At various intervals during the day, tighten these muscles for three seconds, then release and relax for three seconds.

Repeat the exercise ten times. Try to do the exercises about once an hour, and increase the repetitions to as many as you have time for. Some doctors recommend five minutes of Kegels each hour, or about 50 repetitions.

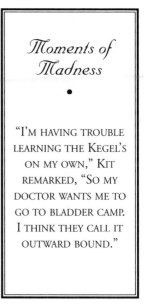

Moments of Madness

•

"I'M HAVING TROUBLE LEARNING THE KEGEL'S ON MY OWN," KIT REMARKED, "SO MY DOCTOR WANTS ME TO GO TO BLADDER CAMP. I THINK THEY CALL IT OUTWARD BOUND."

If your stress incontinence problem is severe, it may take a few months for these exercises to fully have an effect. In minor cases, the exercises are effective almost immediately.

Using traditional medicine.—The traditional surgical approach for stress incontinence involves resuspension of the bladder to help restore the normal angle between it and the urethra. The use of the ring or pessary in the presence of vaginal or uterine prolapse is another option (see page 156). A more recent repair option involves collagen injections strategically placed on either side of the urethra.

Restoring the estrogen levels in muscles and connective tissues of the body improves and at times eliminates many of these problems. If incontinence is a problem for you, ask your doctor if hormone replacement is a good treatment.

Medications benefit some women. Among the options are:

For overflow incontinence: bethanechol (Urecholine®), tera-zosin (Hytrin®), prazosin (Minipress®);

For stress incontinence: phenylpropanolamine (Dimetapp®), pseudephedrine (Sudafed®), imipramine (Hanimine®, Tofranil®), estrogen intravaginal cream (Estrace®, Premarin®);

For urge incontinence: oxybutynin (Ditropan®), flavoxate (Urispas®), imipramine (Janimine®, Tofranil®), estrogen intravaginal cream (Estrace®, Premarin®), oral estrogen (Premarin), transdermal estrogen (Estraderm®), nifedipine (Procardia®).

Other possibilities.—Sometimes the cause for incontinence can be simple, like not going to the bathroom when you first feel the need. Sometimes the cure can likewise be simple: learn to listen to and act on nature's call.

Bladder training can help you control your body's voiding reflex. It involves teaching yourself to urinate at fixed times. To begin training your bladder, visit the bathroom every 30 minutes to an hour, then gradually increase the time between trips in five-minute intervals. Continue this training for six weeks to several months.

Keep a diary of how often you void, how often you leak, and what you are doing at the time of the incontinent episode. There is probably a pattern. If you find you are wet every hour or two, empty your bladder as completely as you can every 30 to 60 minutes. Try to stop the urge to void at unscheduled times by distracting yourself or relaxing. Then void on your schedule. If you cannot wait until the scheduled time, void as needed as completely as possible, but void again at the sched-uled time.

This training is difficult; it takes time, patience, and persistence. Reward yourself for staying on schedule, and look forward to the resolution of the incontinence problem.

Finally, in addition to the basic Kegel exercises, there are some variations that help strengthen pelvic muscles. One of them is to contract and release the pelvic floor muscles as rapidly as you can. This feels like a muscle flutter and should be repeated 25 to 30 times daily, working up to 200 a day. Another is the gradual tensing of the muscles, beginning with an anal contraction and moving forward and upward to the vaginal area. Gradually tighten and then gradually relax each muscle. Repeat this six times. Try to do the complete set of six contractions and releases at least three times each day.

MEMORY LOSS

Joanie walked to the base of the stairway and headed up. She was almost halfway up when she stopped in her tracks. "What am I going up here for?" she said aloud to no one. She hesitated on the stairs for almost five full minutes trying to think what she needed upstairs. "I know I needed something up here, but I just can't think what it was. I'm really losing it."

Estrogen plays a role in the way the brain makes connections. When estrogen supplies are unpredictable, the brain seems to short-circuit at times, particularly in relation to short-term memory. You may remember ancient history but you tend to lose that thought you had five minutes before. In tests in menopausal women, those taking estrogen had fewer short-term memory difficulties than those who were not given the hormone.

Moments of Madness

•

SEEN ON A T-SHIRT:

JUST WHEN I GOT MY ACT TOGETHER, I FORGOT WHERE I PUT IT.

What can you do about it?

Helping yourself.—When you must remember, take a tape recorder to important meetings and record everything for replay later. Use notes and calendars to remind yourself of everything that must be done. Ask your coworkers for the help if you're concerned about what was said or done, and don't expect too much of yourself. Everyone forgets at times.

Using traditional medicine.—Scientific evidence supports the theory that hormone replacement therapy can improve short-term memory and improve other mental functions as well.

Other possibilities.— There are some tricks you can learn to train yourself to remember. For example, mnemonic devices help some people remember words or names. For instance, Claude Raines is a simple name to remember, because Claude could become Cloud and a rainstorm coming from that cloud could trigger "Raines." With practice, you can call up this picture every time you try to remember Claude Raines.

Another tool is to jot down names of new acquaintances and note something you associate with them. If your new acquaintance, Sharon, likes quilting, write "Sharon quilts" on your name list. Make lists for other things that you have trouble remembering. If it's appointments, carry a calendar. If it's shopping or errands, keep lists. Think of these as "memory challenges" and don't let them frustrate you.

MENTAL FUZZINESS

Sylvia, a vice president of an advertising agency, sat at her desk. She knew she had the perfect slogan for the new fruit drink that her clients were introducing to the market. She had even spoken it aloud that morning when the idea struck her in a flash of brilliance. But now, try as she might, she couldn't think of it. "What am I going to do?" she thought. "I feel like I'm losing my mind."

Research has shown that estrogen stimulates production of specific chemical messengers involved in thinking and memory. When estrogen levels wane, chemical balances in the brain are disturbed and the phenomenon of "fuzzy thinking" occurs for some women.

What can you do about fuzzy thinking?

Helping yourself.—Be alert to the possibility that you might have days when your thinking is not as focused as you would like. If you're feeling fuzzy, be patient with yourself and take the breaks you need to feel stabilized again. If critical tasks must be performed, make a list of the steps involved, and check them off to be sure nothing is overlooked. Better yet, ask for help or backup. It's better to be honest up front and confess you're not feeling your best than to risk making critical errors.

Using traditional medicine.—Even though we are still fuzzy about how estrogen and brain chemicals work together, we know enough to be able to say that intellectual and memory function often stabilize with hormone therapy.

At Rockefeller University in New York City, researchers have shown that estrogen has a definite effect on the number of brain connections in the brains of rats. Granted, human brains are far different from those of rats, but this evidence has led to the conclusion that a decrease in estrogen in the brains of human beings leads to "a decline in cognitive performance."

We don't want you to think that this entire book is a pitch for hormone thera-

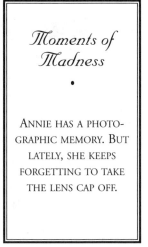

Moments of Madness

•

ANNIE HAS A PHOTO-GRAPHIC MEMORY. BUT LATELY, SHE KEEPS FORGETTING TO TAKE THE LENS CAP OFF.

py, but you do need to know the facts, and this is one more case where hormone replacement usually reverses symptoms.

Other possibilities.—Biofeedback training is helpful for some women who have problems with mental fuzziness. This is an electronic approach for controlling your own brain waves. You learn to recognize certain brain states by reading the "feedback" on an electroencephalogram—a graph of your brain waves. You then can relate how you feel with what you see on the printout.

With practice, you can learn to change your brain states at will. By inducing relaxation, for example, you'll sleep more soundly and have fewer periods of fuzzy thinking—at least in theory.

Vitamin E, vitamin C, and bioflavonoids, all available in health-food stores, also have been reported as alleviating mental fuzziness in a number of women.

MIGRAINE HEADACHES

(See Headaches)

MOOD SWINGS

Sara went to her doctor to get some help. She was in her perimenopausal years and had several small children at home, all very demanding. The doctor gave her a prescription for Valium® and sent her home. At her next appointment, the doctor asked how she was getting along on the Valium. "I'm doing great. Things are wonderful, but what do you mean, how am I doing on the Valium? I thought it was for the kids!"

Mood swings, irritability, depression, insomnia, forgetfulness, anxiety . . . the list alone evokes strong emotions. Mood swings are yet another marker of the perimenopause. Some experts say the mood shifts are usually linked with lack of sleep, while others believe they are directly related to hormonal changes.

Research shows that estrogen and androgens (testosterone in particular) play a role in regulating moods and promoting a sense of well-being. Estrogen also probably affects a number of neurotransmitters that trigger feelings of depression and euphoria. For example, estrogen is thought to reduce levels of monoamine oxidase (MAO), a brain chemical. Lower levels of MAO lead to higher levels of catecholamines. The higher the levels of the catecholamines, the better you feel. So when you're short of estrogen, you may also be short on catecholamines.

There's still a lot of research needed to understand the complex brain chemicals and their relationship to estrogen, but one thing is certain. Estrogen definitely promotes good sleep, and when mood swings are related to sleeplessness, you're bound to feel better when you get more sleep.

What can you do about mood swings?

Helping yourself.—Some active ways of dealing with mood swings include keeping a journal of your feelings, reading about or sharing information with other women, and studying psychology. This could be the time to take advantage of a great learning experience. Try to discover which behaviors trigger mood swings, what sets you off, and what calms you down. Despite the hormonal upheavals taking place in your body, you can take control of many mood fluctuations and learn a lot about yourself at the same time.

Above all, stay calm and know that this may well be normal. When depression feels overwhelming, remind yourself that tomorrow the sun will shine again, and you'll probably feel on top of the world. But always get help if you feel frightened.

Using traditional medicine.—Mood swings related to menopause often disappear with hormone replacement therapy—as well as without it for some women. If, however, you are clinically depressed or have another illness that is unrelated to hormones, it is important to get medical attention.

Other possibilities.—If coping with ordinary events is just too difficult, consider seeing a psychologist or joining a support group. Working with others often helps restore your perspective on your own mood swings. Remember, the term is swing. Expect to be up and then down. If you anticipate some shifts, the feelings probably won't be overwhelming.

NAUSEA

(See Digestive Distresses)

Just a note here: Some women do experience nausea in the early days of hormone therapy. This is transitory and passes as quickly as your body adjusts to its new levels of estrogen. If nausea persists, however, see your doctor to talk about what is going on. If nausea is accompanied by weight loss or dehydration, it is quite possibly a signal that something more serious is going on, and you'll want to know what it is.

NEGATIVE THINKING

(See Depression and Mood Swings)

NERVOUSNESS

(See Anxiety, Mood Swings, and Stress)

NIGHT SWEATS

Pat woke up drenched. Her sheets were soaking wet and her night clothes were dripping. "Unbelievable!" she gasped. "It's only 35° outside, and I've become a sleeping sauna. What's the deal?"

Night sweats are essentially hot flashes that occur during sleep. They are yet another of those "vasomotor instability" symptoms that occur with fluctuating hormone levels. Like the hot flash, no one knows exactly what precipitates night sweats, but they are believed to be related to an unregulated release of hormones from the hypothalamus and pituitary.

What can you do about night sweats?

Helping yourself.—Changing clothes and maybe even changing the sheets might make you more comfortable. Then treat yourself to a soothing cup of bedtime tea and try to get back to sleep.

Using traditional medicine.—Hormone replacement therapy is effective in counteracting the hot flashes and flushing that usually trigger night sweats. Many women choose to simply live through this time of their lives. Eventually the night sweats disappear, along with hot flashes.

Other possibilities.—If you cannot take estrogen, there are other medications that may be of benefit. Clonidine, progesterone, Bellergal, Rejuvex®, Femtrol®, herbal preparations (especially dong quai and ginseng), and androgens sometimes help. Read more about these alternative therapies in the section about Hot Flashes on page 88.

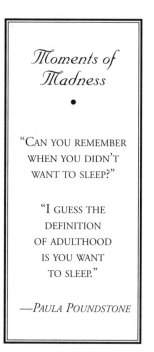

Moments of Madness

•

"CAN YOU REMEMBER WHEN YOU DIDN'T WANT TO SLEEP?"

"I GUESS THE DEFINITION OF ADULTHOOD IS YOU WANT TO SLEEP."

—*PAULA POUNDSTONE*

OSTEOPOROSIS

(Because this problem is so important, we've devoted a major part of Chapter 5 to it. See pages 183-188.)

OVERSENSITIVITY

(See Mood Swings)

PAIN WITH INTERCOURSE

Jody lost all interest in sex. Oh, she wasn't completely frigid. It was just that the last few times she'd tried to have intercourse, it caused a painful, burning sensation that was far from pleasurable. The pain was so intense, she had to ask her husband to stop, and this created some conflict.

As estrogen sources become scarce, tissues in the body dry out and lose elasticity. This is especially true for the delicate tissues of the vagina. The friction created by this lack of lubrication causes pain.

What can you do to resume a normal sex life?

Helping yourself.—Lubricating creams or gels help. A number of vaginal lubricants are available over the counter at the pharmacy. Read the ingredients, and select one that does not contain alcohol. Alcohol can increase dryness, leading to more discomfort.

Using traditional medicine.—Hormone replacement usually alleviates the problem. The vaginal dryness that causes pain with intercourse will resolve once there is enough estrogen back in your body to remoisturize those tissues. Oral hormones may not be enough at the beginning, so ask your doctor about vaginal creams that contain estrogen. These can bring more immediate relief.

Other possibilities.—It is important to remember that the enjoyment of sex doesn't need to diminish, let alone disappear, with age. In healthy women, some form of sexual appetite is present throughout life. As a matter of fact, the Duke Center for the Study of Aging and Human Development, which began in 1954, found that interest and capacity for sexual activity existed well into the ninth decade of life.

Dr. Theodore Brooks, writing in the March 1994 journal *The Female Patient,* states: "Contrary to the prevailing stereotype, many menopausal and postmenopausal women report heightened libido—possibly as a function of unopposed testosterone and lowered estrogen levels . . . ." His conclusion: "Attitude is everything." If you take care of yourself and have positive self-esteem, you'll enjoy your sexuality.

PANIC ATTACKS

(See Anxiety)

POSTMENOPAUSAL VAGINAL BLEEDING

Wendy had been taking estrogen and progesterone for six months. Her periods had disappeared over a year ago, and now, out of the blue, she began to bleed. She figured it was just her periods returning since she started hormone therapy. But when the bleeding had not stopped after two weeks, she called the doctor.

Bleeding after menopause is always considered abnormal until proven otherwise. This means you need to see a doctor immediately if it occurs. Don't wait two weeks like Wendy did.

Most often, the cause of this breakthrough bleeding is not serious. But if left untreated, it can become serious. Usually the bleeding is a result of the buildup of blood in the walls of the uterus. Sometimes it can be stopped with additional progesterone.

Other possible causes of bleeding include atrophic vaginitis, noncancerous endometrial or cervical polyps, and endometrial hyperplasia. Endometrial hyperplasia is the medical term for the overgrowth of endometrial cells. This overgrowth is often the result of stimulation by estrogen and, while it may be inconvenient, it is usually not life-threatening.

More serious, however, is the possibility that endometrial cancer is present. Since this is treatable, women who might have it should undergo a series of diagnostic tests, including pelvic ultrasound, endometrial sampling, hysteroscopy, and dilation and curettage (D & C). Many times, benign polyps are responsible for the bleeding. But don't take any chances. Early detection and intervention is the key to survival and recovery from any cancer.

What should you do about breakthrough bleeding?

Helping yourself.—Always consult your doctor. Delay only intensifies your worry. We repeat: Any bleeding after menopause should be considered abnormal.

Using traditional medicine.—Breakthrough bleeding is the single most important early indication of endometrial cancer. Almost all women with endometrial cancer will experience abnormal bleeding, but if detected early, nearly all precancerous cases can be cured.

The tests you'll want to undergo include:

- Endometrial sampling
- Ultrasound, either abdominal or vaginal
- Color doppler ultrasound
- Hysteroscopy
- Dilation and curettage (D & C)

Discuss each of these with your doctor. While the entire battery of tests is usually not necessary, the list suggests the full range of possibilities.

If, for example, you believe that the discomfort of having a full bladder, as is required for an abdominal ultrasound, will be more than you can handle, ask for a vaginal ultrasound. Your doctor should be able to inform you about each of the procedures, but if you are not getting sufficient information, ask lots of questions. And by all means, seek a second opinion if you still have concerns.

NOTE: If you are taking estrogens and progesterone in a sequential, cyclic fashion, you may experience some normal and predictable withdrawal bleeding. Discuss this possibility with your gynecologist.

Other possibilities.—Sometimes bleeding after menopause may be cervical, vulvar, or vaginal instead of uterine. Having a regular Pap smear is one of the most effective ways to detect serious problems in their earliest stages.

In addition to your regular gynecological exam, learn to perform a genital self-examination. Then do this exam once a month. This simple examination is a key to early diagnosis and treatment of vulvar cancer, which may not be accompanied by bleeding. A raised sore that may be ulcerated, white, or wart-like is sometimes present with this disease.

The self-exam requires only that you use a hand-held mirror and a good light to look at your vaginal area. Any abnormalities should be called to your doctor's attention. Vulvar cancer is usually curable if caught early enough.

PREMENSTRUAL SYNDROME (PMS)

Diane tried to find something healthy to eat to satisfy what seemed to be an insatiable desire for sweets. She knew she would lose, however, and after eating half a dozen fat-free fig Newtons, drinking two glasses of skim milk, and consuming two peaches, she still wanted chocolate. Diane also knew that for the next five days, she'd feel weepy and bloated and have headaches. It was her monthly bout with premenstrual syndrome.

PMS and its causes have been the subject of lively debate. Theories have implicated estrogen, progesterone, fatty acids, prostaglandins, prolactin, and serotonin, among other possible causes. One thing is certain: PMS is real, and for some women, it can be very serious. At the very least, it creates emotional havoc. Sadly, there is no cure for it yet.

PMS symptoms may increase as you approach menopause. Symptoms can range from physical pain to intense anger and depression. The symptoms alone aren't quite as important in helping to confirm a PMS diagnosis as is the cyclical nature and the clustering of the presentation of these symptoms.

What can you do about PMS?

Helping yourself.—Because PMS symptoms are cyclical, it is important that you keep a daily diary of how you feel, physically and emotionally, during this time of your life.

Keep track of your periods, however sporadic they may be, and try to pinpoint the relationship of mood swings to ovulation. Also note things like hunger, headaches, cramps, bloating, and depression. This will help both you and your doctor get a handle on the severity of your symptoms and what to do about them.

Using traditional medicine.—Accurately diagnosing PMS is the greatest challenge in managing it. The tests you'll want to have your doctor order for you should include thyroid function (TSH, T4, TRH), prolactin, complete blood cell count (CBC), liver enzymes, chlamydia (both culture and antibody testing), androgen measurements, and follicle-stimulating hormone (FSH) and luteinizing hormone (LH) values.

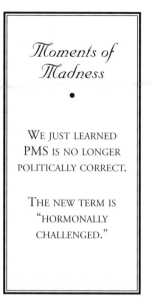

Moments of Madness

•

WE JUST LEARNED PMS IS NO LONGER POLITICALLY CORRECT.

THE NEW TERM IS "HORMONALLY CHALLENGED."

Many medical options are available. Depending on the specific symptoms, your doctor may prescribe nonsteroidal anti-inflammatory drugs (NSAIDs) such as Advil® or Motrin®. Or antibiotic therapy might be appropriate if some condition like pelvic inflammatory disease (PID) is suspected. Oral contraceptives have also been used and are known to help about 25 percent of the time.

The most effective drugs identified to date include Danacrine®, progesterone, and a gonadotropin-releasing hormone agent given in the form of daily shots for part of the monthly cycle. The latter, in combination with hormone replacement therapy, generally is used only when PMS is severe and unresponsive to other types of treatment.

If your symptoms are severe and nothing seems to help, your doctor might suggest hysterectomy. Because of the implications of this surgery on your later life, you will want to consider this option only if all else fails and you are really miserable.

Other possibilities.—Your doctor may suggest psychoactive drugs if your symptoms of anxiety or agitation are most bothersome.

In addition, many women believe these options help.

- Exercise every day;

- Increase your intake of complex carbohydrates and protein (vegetables, whole grains, fish), and decrease your intake of salt and refined sugars;

- Eat small, frequent meals;

- Avoid caffeine and alcohol;

- Participate in some kind of group therapy for emotional support.

PMS usually disappears once your periods stop or when hormone replacement or therapy is begun.

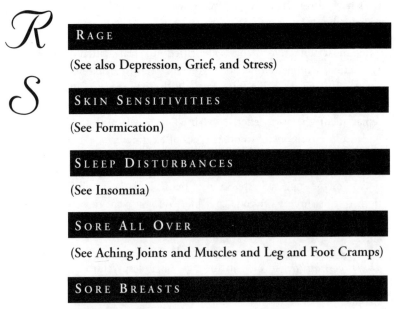

RAGE

(See also Depression, Grief, and Stress)

SKIN SENSITIVITIES

(See Formication)

SLEEP DISTURBANCES

(See Insomnia)

SORE ALL OVER

(See Aching Joints and Muscles and Leg and Foot Cramps)

SORE BREASTS

(See Breast Changes)

SPOTTING

Spotting is an unusually light menstrual flow. It may occur a day or two before you would normally expect your period, or it may occur at unpredictable times. It is often the result of anovulation—a menstrual cycle in which your ovaries did not release an egg.

Spotting is common during the perimenopausal years, and as you approach menopause, it may occur more frequently. If spotting occurs more than a year after menopause, it should be considered abnormal until proven otherwise. (See also Postmenopausal Vaginal Bleeding on page 107.)

What can you do about spotting?

Helping yourself.—The most important thing to do about spotting is be sure to report it to your doctor. If spotting is an indication that you are not ovulating, it is not in itself a serious problem. But studies have shown that women of reproductive age who don't ovulate for a prolonged period of time may experience the same bone loss as postmenopausal women. This means you may be at risk for osteoporosis later in life.

Using traditional medicine.—All menstrual irregularities should be reported to your doctor, and spotting is no exception. If spotting occurs instead of your regular period, you and your doctor will want to find out why. If it occurs in addition to a regular period, it may indicate the presence of other problems.

As with other menstrual irregularities, hormone replacement is helpful for many women. Discuss this with your doctor.

If you miss a period altogether, your doctor will want to rule out one of the main causes: pregnancy. You can still get pregnant during the perimenopausal years. If you know you are not pregnant, and if you don't have periods for several months, ask your doctor to test for FSH (follicle-stimulating hormone) levels to see if you are menopausal and for estrogen levels to determine if you are estrogen deficient. Your doctor will also want to do a pelvic examination to rule out the possibility of ovarian cysts that could be interfering with regular menstruation.

Other possibilities.—If you are not pregnant and if there are no ovarian cysts interfering with menstruation, your doctor will need to look for other causes. These may include thyroid problems, stress, extreme weight changes, and over-training with exercise.

STRESS

(Including nervousness, depression, and rage)

Bobbie didn't think she was "stressed out." She felt as though she was coping pretty well, despite her recent divorce, the troubles with her teenage son, and the fact that she lost her job. She was still functioning. But her periods stopped, and she was only 43. She had terrible migraine headaches and was losing weight, even though she ate everything in sight. When she finally saw her doctor, they spent the whole time talking about her stress.

Most of us know what stress feels like. It can be generated by job changes, family arguments, relocation, work pressures, or many other factors, including changes occurring around menopause. Stress is known to affect overall physical health, as well as the endocrine system and the immune system. People who experience chronic stress are likely to have more colds, more headaches, and more gastrointestinal problems. And, of course, stress is implicated in the development of more serious illnesses, including heart disease, high blood pressure, arthritis, peptic ulcers, and even cancer.

To understand stress, we need to look at the individual "stressors." What is causing the pressure? Taken individually, one challenge probably won't affect your overall health. But for many women, the midlife stress load is often well beyond what anyone might be expected to handle.

What can you do to cope better?

Technically, the stress response in the body can occur as a result of any disturbance: heat or cold, environmental toxins, microorganisms, physical trauma, or strong emotional reactions. All of these can trigger the physical response recognized as the "stress response."

Biologically, what happens in the body is pretty much controlled and regulated by the endocrine system, mostly by the adrenal glands. When the body is confronted with acute stress, a surge of adrenaline helps you to escape danger.

In the case of chronic stress, however, the adrenal glands secrete cortisol, a substance that raises blood cholesterol and triglyceride levels and causes your body to hang on to its supply of salt.

Chronic overstressing of the adrenal glands can lead to depressed immune function, chronic fatigue, low blood sugar, allergies, and chronic infections, among other conditions.

Helping yourself.—It stands to reason, then, that protecting and supporting the adrenal glands is important during the

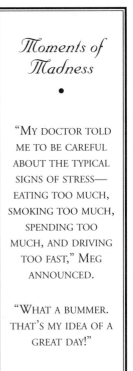

Moments of Madness

•

"MY DOCTOR TOLD ME TO BE CAREFUL ABOUT THE TYPICAL SIGNS OF STRESS— EATING TOO MUCH, SMOKING TOO MUCH, SPENDING TOO MUCH, AND DRIVING TOO FAST," MEG ANNOUNCED.

"WHAT A BUMMER. THAT'S MY IDEA OF A GREAT DAY!"

perimenopausal years. One of the best ways to do this is by dealing with stress effectively. That means you'll want to eliminate any negative coping strategies that cause more harm than good over the long haul. Examples are:

- dependence on chemicals
- overeating
- smoking
- watching too much television
- using too much alcohol

These behaviors, among many others, can be replaced with more positive approaches, such as:

- using relaxation exercises
- scheduling regular physical exercise
- practicing diaphragmatic breathing techniques
- taking time for prayer and meditation
- learning progressive relaxation
- trying biofeedback
- using positive self-talk or self-hypnosis
- joining a support group

All of these approaches have been found to have positive effects—not just on how you cope with stress, but on your physical health as well.

Using traditional medicine.—When feelings of depression, anxiety, rage, and panic don't disappear even with positive coping strategies, be sure to talk with your doctor. Depression is a serious medical condition with biochemical, genetic, and environmental causes. It can be treated.

There are two medically recognized forms of stress-related depression: major depression and manic-depressive illness. Major depression is quite common around midlife and later. It can occur just once or recur many times. Physical symptoms associated with depression include appetite disturbances, headaches, digestive disorders, and chronic pain.

Manic-depressive illness is less common than major depression. With this disorder, a period of depression is followed by a strange sense of euphoria or increased energy. This illness can include all of the physical symptoms of major depression but then symptoms suddenly change to periods of elation, irritability, insomnia, and poor judgment, among others.

Both of these forms of illness need medical treatment. If you feel your stress is out of control, see a doctor. Be sure to tell him or her about any family history of such illnesses. If possible, keep a journal of your feelings to help you sort through exactly what might be happening.

Other possibilities.—Diet can be an important part of managing stress. Evidence suggests you can counterbalance some of the anxiety associated with stress with what you eat. A meal containing carbohydrates, for example, is known to raise brain levels of an amino acid called tryptophan. Tryptophan is converted to serotonin, which controls hormone secretions, sleep, and how we perceive pain. Serotonin is a natural substance that calms us down.

Along with eating right, you should try to exercise regularly. Regular physical activity, preferably something aerobic like walking, bicycling, or swimming, triggers production of a group of hormones called endorphins. These hormones put you into a state of natural relaxation and provide a very dependable way to manage stress.

Finally, always get plenty of rest. If stress is interfering with sleep, talk to your doctor. Fatigue can interfere with even the best efforts to manage stress.

SUICIDAL THOUGHTS

(See Depression and Stress)

URINARY INCONTINENCE

(See Loss of Urinary Control or Bladder Changes)

VAGINAL DRYNESS AND ITCHING

No matter what Penny did, she was not comfortable. The terrible itching and subsequent embarrassment and pain from scratching left her in turmoil. She thought she had some horrible sexually transmitted disease. When she could tolerate the itching no longer, she went to see her gynecologist.

Penny learned that what she was experiencing was really not unusual. During the perimenopausal years, as estrogen stores wane, tissues in every part of the body begin to dry out. The tissues in the vaginal area are more susceptible to dryness, though, because they are wiped and dried with toilet paper after each trip to the bathroom.

What can you do about vaginal dryness and itching?

Helping yourself.—To help prevent vaginal itching from becoming a serious problem, don't hesitate to discuss it with your doctor. Try to use soft paper products that are a bit more gentle on these delicate tissues. Dry, rough papers can make the problem worse and set you up for potential infections.

Using traditional medicine.—Estrogen cream goes right to the source of the problem and can be obtained with a prescription. Because the cream is applied directly to the area that needs it, relief usually comes quickly.

Estrogen creams, when used in a low dose are considered very safe. Even women with a family history of breast cancer can consider using them. However, keep in mind that estrogen creams used for vaginal itching are absorbed into the bloodstream. You should talk with your doctor about just how much to use if you are already taking oral estrogen.

NOTE: Over time, as the vaginal tissues become healthier, more estrogen will be absorbed from the vagina and will circulate throughout the body.

Other possibilities.—The sole disadvantage of estrogen vaginal creams is that they are messy. To protect clothing, many women suggest wearing a panty liner.

An estrogen vaginal insert now in use in Europe is not absorbed into the bloodstream, so the therapeutic effect of the estrogen is limited to the vaginal area. This may be safer for some women. Watch for it to become available in the United States and by all means alert your doctor to the fact that it should be coming.

Water Retention

Emily started hormone replacement therapy after her insomnia and hot flashes finally got the best of her. After the first few days, she began to have that premenstrual bloated feeling, and she saw the scale creep up, first one pound, then two more. "Wait just a minute," she wailed. "I thought hormones made all these problems disappear. What's happening now?"

Fluid retention is the most commonly reported side effect among women taking progesterone as part of hormone replacement therapy. The water retention usually lasts only a few weeks or months.

What can you do about water retention?

Helping yourself.—The best defense against retaining water is to drink it. Drink eight to ten glasses of water daily. This acts as a natural diuretic and keeps your system well flushed. Avoid salt whenever you can, since salt helps your body retain fluid.

Using traditional medicine.—If the problem becomes severe or lasts beyond a few months, discuss the possibility of taking less progesterone with the doctor. Sometimes a diuretic (water pill) can be prescribed to help you over the most uncomfortable times.

If you do take a diuretic, try to eat plenty of potassium-rich foods, like bananas. Diuretics tend to flush out potassium along with extra water.

Other possibilities.—Get plenty of regular aerobic exercise. Increasing your muscle mass and decreasing the fat seems to reduce the body's need to store water.

WEAKNESS OR FATIGUE

(See Fatigue)

WEIGHT GAIN

Nancy was a dancer. She spent most of her waking hours pursuing some fitness activity. She didn't weigh herself frequently because she really didn't need to. Her weight had been stable for years. Then she started to notice that she was putting on some extra weight—not all at once, but a little at a time. And she found she couldn't get the weight off. By the time she was 50, she had added 10 pounds . . . not so bad for most women, but it really bothered Nancy.

The biggest complaint among women during the menopausal years is related to weight gain. Without any change in activity or eating behavior, many women gain weight during these years. There is an explanation, or at least a theory.

As the ovaries slow down their production of estrogen, the body is busy producing estrone, an estrogen-like chemical that is manufactured in fat cells. As the body uses this estrone, the pituitary gets a signal to produce more fat cells where estrone could be manufactured. While this is currently just a theory, we offer it here as a possible explanation for why so many women gain weight during the perimenopausal years.

There is some good news, though. Studies have shown that women who are at least ten pounds heavier at age 45 than they were at age 35 have an easier transition during the peri-menopausal years. Heavier women usually have a later menopause, fewer and less severe hot flashes, and denser bones than their thinner counterparts.

Women who start hormone replacement therapy also tend to gain weight. There is no scientific evidence at this time to ver-ify this or refute it. But, there is some evidence that body weight may be redistributed. The fatty tissue of the buttocks and breasts may seem to move around to the waistline.

A slow-down in metabolism is a perfectly normal part of aging. As we get older, we need fewer calories to keep us going. A moderately active, 5-foot, 4-inch 35-year-old women who weighs around 130 pounds needs about 1800 calories a day. By the time she is 60, she will burn only 1600 calories a day. Without a change in her daily food intake, she will store an extra 200 calories every day.

What can you do about weight gain?

Helping yourself.—The most important advice about weight gain during this time is "Cut yourself some slack!" Don't cen-ter your life around being on a diet. Most, if not all, diets don't work and many, in fact, are harmful. Instead, adopt an eating and exercise style that will sustain you for the rest of your life. Choose a plan that fits your lifestyle and provides you with all the nutrients you need for good health. A very important dietary change is to limit your intake of fat, since fat only begets fat in the body.

Choose an exercise plan that meets the goals of your changing life. Use weight-bearing exercise to build muscle tissue and strengthen bones and aerobic exercise to oxygenate your body and strengthen your heart. Doing some combination of both of these for 20 to 40 minutes daily, five times a week, is optimal.

Using traditional medicine.—If you are more than about 10 percent over your ideal body weight (see chart on page 206), you may want to consider some medical intervention to help you manage your weight. The famous Framingham study has shown that being as little as 10 percent overweight can lead to a higher incidence of heart disease and death from all causes.

Losing weight is very difficult for many women. If you are seriously concerned, ask your doctor, dietitian, or other health care professional for advice and help.

Other possibilities.—There are over-the-counter appetite suppressants that may be tempting but should be avoided. Any efforts to lose weight without nutritional training and behavior modification are usually futile. Powdered food substitutes work only temporarily. When women using this weight-loss method return to real food, most gain back all they lost and sometimes more.

Using nationally recognized support programs like Weight Watchers can be helpful. Again, be sure part of the program includes behavior modification training, and don't expect to lose weight permanently without including exercise as a daily activity.

Yeast Infections

Jane had gone to the doctor for treatment of her sore throat. She took antibiotics for 10 days, but then a new and more troublesome problem appeared. Every time Jane urinated, she felt a painful, burning sensation. She went back to the doctor only to learn that the antibiotics had created a certain imbalance in her body, causing a yeast infection.

Some antibiotics destroy normal bacteria in the body at the same time as they kill the germs that make us sick. When the bacteria are wiped out, however, yeasts, specifically *candida albicans,* are likely to move in unchecked.

What can you do about yeast infections?

Helping yourself.—If you must take antibiotics (and we all need to at one time or another), you might consider eating yogurt frequently during the antibiotic course. Yogurt helps keep normal bacteria levels up to counteract yeast growth.

Using traditional medicine.—If you know you're sensitive to antibiotics and have had yeast infections before, be sure your doctor knows this. Penicillin and most other antibiotics like erythromycin, which attack germs found in the nose, throat, and lungs, are likely to cause problems and activate vaginal yeast.

If you have a history of yeast infections, ask your doctor about antifungal drugs that kill yeasts and yeast-like fungi. Some are available without prescription.

Moments of Madness

•

"My husband went to one of those workshops where men try to get in touch with their feminine side," Abbey told us.

"Poor guy came home with a terrible yeast infection."

Other possibilities.—*Candida albicans,* the common yeast (also known as an allergenic microbe) that may cause a depressed immune reaction in some sensitive people, is found in every human body. A relationship has been found between many chronic illnesses and this common yeast.

Some symptoms that are believed to be associated with an overgrowth of *c. albicans* include headaches, fatigue, depression, irritability, digestive disorders, respiratory disorders, joint pains, menstrual disorders, skin rashes, recurrent bladder and vaginal infections, and sensitivity to odors and additives.

While the list is long, the treatment is fairly simple. Notice how many of the symptoms also occur with menopause. If your menopausal symptoms don't resolve with hormone replacement therapy, ask your doctor to let you try something like Nystatin® or Monistat®, which are very effective for chronic yeast infections.

ZITS

(See Acne)

SUMMING UP

If you're reading this book cover to cover, by now you should be exhausted. While this list may feel overwhelming, there probably are even a few more problems women deal with at midlife that we haven't touched on here. We didn't set out to provide an in-depth resource on menopause. Instead our goal is to introduce some of the changes we know many women wonder about.

Your library, local bookstore, or health care facility should be able to help you get more information. Learn all you can so you can be in control during these important years.

$\mathcal{T}$HE HORMONE EXPRESS: WILL WE RIDE FOREVER?

$\mathcal{I}$f you painstakingly worked your way through Chapter 2, you know that the signs and symptoms of menopause outnumber Liz Taylor's husbands by a huge margin. And you also probably noticed that hormone replacement therapy (HRT) is mentioned as a solution for many of the discomforts associated with menopause.

This chapter summarizes what we know, what we don't know, and who should and who shouldn't take various hormones.

WHAT WE KNOW ABOUT HRT

In the 1960s, estrogen became famous as an elixir that promised to keep women young and feminine forever. Doctors prescribed it for any woman who wanted it, regardless of menopausal status. Then, in 1975, researchers linked estrogen to uterine cancer, and its use declined dramatically. The aftermath of this was that even women who desperately needed estrogen couldn't get it. The debate over the safety and effectiveness of hormone replacement therapy raged throughout the 1980s.

Today we know that estrogen replacement therapy, used properly in the correct dosage, is safe and effective for the relief of many menopausal symptoms. The U.S. Food and Drug

Administration (FDA) has approved estrogen for the following three conditions:

1. Hot flashes and night sweats (otherwise called "vasomotor symptoms")

2. Vaginal dryness (or "atrophic vaginitis")

3. Prevention and treatment of osteoporosis

There is evidence that estrogen replacement also can protect women from heart disease, although the FDA has not yet approved it for this purpose. The American Fertility Society and the American Heart Association recently sponsored a conference of international experts in women's health care to discuss the issue. The conference attendees reached a consensus in favor of estrogen replacement therapy. In short, they concluded that "postmenopausal estrogen therapy has a role in primary prevention of cardiovascular disease in selected women."

The events of the '60s and '70s caused what has become known as the "estrogen scare." When estrogen alone was prescribed in large dosages, the incidence of uterine cancer did go up. However, estrogen itself is not a carcinogen—that is, it does not cause cancer. But used unopposed (that is, without progesterone, the other important female hormone), it can cause changes in the growth of endometrial tissues.

This condition is described as an excessive buildup or proliferation of the cells of the uterine lining. Is this cancer? No, but among certain women who are predisposed to uterine cancer, this condition can become cancer if it is not discovered and treated early.

The studies that demonstrated the link between the increase in uterine cancer and estrogen replacement also helped us realize that too much of a good thing can become a bad thing.

Also, we needed to learn that estrogen isn't the only player in the complex game of hormones and health for women.

The key words in this brief history are SAFE and USED PROPERLY. The estrogen scare led researchers to discover that estrogen is not needed in huge quantities and that in women in whom the uterus is intact, it is preferable to use progesterone along with estrogen. Estrogen thickens the lining of the uterus, while progesterone promotes shedding of that lining, causing it to waste away.

When progesterone is given in sufficient quantities each month along with a minimal dose of estrogen, there is very little likelihood of a buildup of tissue that could lead to cancer. As a matter of fact, hormone replacement therapy taken this way seems to prevent the development of uterine cancer.

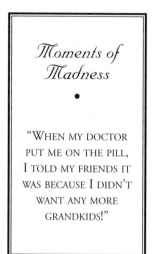

Moments of Madness

•

"WHEN MY DOCTOR PUT ME ON THE PILL, I TOLD MY FRIENDS IT WAS BECAUSE I DIDN'T WANT ANY MORE GRANDKIDS!"

This has been borne out by many studies. In one (Gambrell, Medical College of Georgia, 1983), the incidence of uterine cancer among women who took estrogen with progesterone was only half that of women who took no hormones at all. Another study (Nachtigall, Goldwater Memorial Hospital, New York City, 1973), done on women with unrelated chronic illnesses, showed that after 10 years, no cases of uterine or breast cancer occurred with the combined therapy, whereas both these types of cancer were found in the women who were given a placebo.

Breast cancer is one of the major concerns of all women. In Boston, a study of 5,000 women found fewer cases of breast cancer among those taking hormones than those in the control group (Boston Collaborative Drug Surveillance Study,

1973). A year later, a second study by the same group showed that the incidence of breast cancer was statistically identical among groups of women who did and who did not take hormones. So as it stands, there seems to be no clear link between HRT and breast cancer.

More importantly, Dr. R. Don Gambrell, Jr., of the Medical College of Georgia, the researcher who originally investigated the link between estrogen and endometrial cancer, studied 5,563 postmenopausal women for seven years. His work showed (1) that women on estrogen alone had a lower incidence of breast cancer than women who took no hormones, and (2) that women on both estrogen and progesterone had an incidence even lower than that.

Subsequent studies have hinted at a possible relationship between alcohol use and hormones and breast cancer. But the sample in these studies was extremely small. Much more research is needed before all the questions can be answered.

Here is a summary of what we know so far.

- Breast cancer is the most common kind of cancer found in women. (According to Dr. Peter Ravdin of the University of Texas Health Science Center at San Antonio, 80,000 American women develop node-negative breast cancer every year.)

- Breast cancer is rare in women younger than 30 but becomes more prevalent with age.

- One in every 11 women will have breast cancer during her lifetime.

- A strong family history of breast cancer seems to carry a higher risk. (If your mother had it, your risk is five times higher than that for women with no family history.)

- Women with cystic breasts are at no greater risk of developing breast cancer than those without benign breast lumps, but the chances of missing new lumps increases.

- The risk of breast cancer rises slightly if you reached puberty early or have a late menopause.

- The risk of breast cancer rises slightly if you have never had children.

- The risk of breast cancer decreases if you have breast-fed your children.

Finally, we do know that some cancer cells are what is termed "estrogen-dependent." That means estrogen promotes their growth. Tamoxifen, a drug used to treat breast cancer is "anti-estrogenic." It seems to block estrogen's effect on cancer cells.

The evidence for the link between estrogen and breast cancer dates back to 1943 when some pregnant patients with breast cancer had particularly poor outcomes. Needless to say, everyone is anxiously awaiting more information. Nonetheless, it is very important, in the presence of any kind of cancer, to establish whether the cancer is estrogen dependent and to suspend hormone replacement therapy if the cancer thrives in its presence.

WHAT WE DON'T KNOW ABOUT HRT

What we don't know about hormones and women's bodies could fill volumes. The need for good research is critical. For example, we need more information about exactly how estrogen and progesterone work to stimulate the hypothalamus. Also, we don't know what role estrogen plays in preventing heart disease in women, despite that consensus opinion we talked about earlier. There is evidence that HRT has a positive effect on cholesterol, increasing the high-density lipoprotein

(HDL or "good" cholesterol) and decreasing the low-density lipoprotein (LDL or "bad" cholesterol). But so far we're not sure about exactly what's going on.

A massive evaluation of HRT and heart disease in women, undertaken by the National Institutes of Health, began in 1993 and will continue for nine years. At the end of that time, we hope to know much more.

In late January of 1995, the results of a three-year study called the Postmenopausal Estrogen/Progestin Interventions (PEPI) Trial confirmed that hormone replacement therapy reduces some risk factors for heart disease. This study looked at the effects of estrogen alone, estrogen combined with proges-terone, or a placebo on (1) cholesterol, (2) blood pressure, (3) fibrinogen (a clotting factor), and (4) insulin.

PEPI was set up so the women who took HRT and those who didn't began on an equal basis. It involved 875 healthy post-menopausal women ages 45 to 64, including 278 who had had hysterectomies. All the women were randomly assigned to one of five treatments—daily estrogen plus a natural proges-terone for 12 days a month; daily estrogen plus a synthetic progesterone (progestin) taken 12 days a month; daily estro-gen plus daily progestin; daily unopposed estrogen (estrogen taken alone);or a placebo. Each group had a similar distribu-tion of ages and health histories.

The study found that estrogen, with or without progesterone, raised the levels of HDL cholesterol—the good kind. All hor-mone regimens also significantly lowered LDL or bad choles-terol and fibrinogen levels. None of the hormone treatments used raised blood pressure. The investigation did not last long enough to indicate whether HRT actually reduced heart dis-ease—that is, whether a smaller proportion of women on HRT went on to have heart attacks or strokes. Nor did it show whether HRT prevented osteoporosis or increased the risk of breast cancer. Those questions will be addressed by the 25,000-woman HRT arm of the Women's Health Initiative. Its results won't be in hand for another decade.

Interestingly, when the study ended, all the women weighed more, on average, than they did at the beginning. Those who took placebos gained the most (4.6 pounds). Those who took estrogen alone gained the least (1.5 pounds).

HOW MUCH DO WE NEED?

One of the most important things we don't yet know is exactly what dosages are best. Each woman is unique. At age 10, our bodies are pretty much alike. But by the time we reach age 50, the differences are amazing. And those differences become more evident as we grow still older.

This biological diversity among older women probably explains why researchers used men, not women, as the subjects for the early estrogen studies.

Another thing we don't know is the best way to administer hormones for various women. Are pills right for you, or is an estrogen patch better? Perhaps you need an intramuscular injection. Or should you use a cream? And then should you take the hormones for 25 days, starting progesterone around day 14—or what? No one knows exactly what's best. In fact, there was no science involved in determining how long hormones should be administered each month, either. Today, many experts believe that taking estrogen for the entire month without interruption provides the most convenient relief.

Moments of Madness

•

"I DON'T HAVE ANY SICK DAYS LEFT," MOANED LISA, WHO CONSTANTLY STRUGGLED WITH ACHES AND PAINS. "MAYBE I'LL JUST CALL IN DEAD."

Finally, we don't really know how long women should take hormones. Ten years? An entire lifetime? The jury is still out on this one, and opinions are all over the map. The benefits of the therapy in terms of osteoporosis and bone health in general are well established, but there is some evidence that if you stop taking hormones, whether at age 65 or 75, bones degenerate rather rapidly.

WHO CAN TAKE IT AND WHO CAN'T?

There are some lucky women who never need to take any hormones. These women are blessed with bodies that stop producing estrogen so gradually they never experience the stress of withdrawal.

Then there are those who should not take estrogen because of specific pre-existing conditions. These "contraindications" include the following—but this is by no means a complete list:

- Women with previously diagnosed or suspected breast cancer that is estrogen-dependent;

- Women with active liver disease;

- Women with active thrombophlebitis (blood clots);

- Women with thromboembolic disorders (blood clots that break off and travel to the brain or lungs, causing strokes or pulmonary embolism).

We also have a list of what are known as "relative contraindications." Women with these problems should use hormone therapy only if the benefits significantly outweigh the risks. This group includes:

- Women with chronic liver disorders;

- Those who are markedly obese.

- Women with uterine fibroids;

- Women with a history of thrombophlebitis or embolism;

- Those with a history of endometriosis;

- Women who have had endometrial cancer;

- Those with a history of breast cancer.

So, who should take estrogen? Theoretically, everyone else. Evidence is mounting that estrogen can be a wonder drug for many women.

One group that seems to benefit greatly is women who are prime candidates for osteoporosis. With this disorder, the bones become thin and fragile. After menopause, bone loss occurs in all women, but for those with a strong family history, the loss can be irreversible. (See Chapter 5 for details about osteoporosis and a personal risk assessment form to help you determine your susceptibility.)

The women who tend to benefit most from hormone replacement therapy are those with uncomfortable menopausal symptoms. If your symptoms affect your quality of life, it probably is time to talk with your doctors about hormones.

Finally, women with family histories of heart disease, atherosclerosis, or hardening of the arteries should strongly consider hormone replacement.

The recent studies on hormone therapy using low doses of estrogen combined with progesterone present a strong case for estrogen replacement for most women. Learn all you can and then talk with your doctor about what is best for you.

Are there side effects?

Yes, some women do have side effects with hormone replacement therapy. They don't affect everyone, but you need to know what they are

The possible side effects of the estrogen include:

—Nausea

—Breast tenderness

—Fluid retention

—Breakthrough bleeding

—Slight increase in the incidence of gallstones

The possible side effects of progesterone include:

—Abdominal bloating

—Headaches

—Breast pain

—Nervousness

—Continuation of menstrual bleeding

—Depression, mood changes, PMS-like symptoms

Some of those sound pretty grim, but remember, they don't affect all women. Doses can usually be adjusted to counteract the side effects. These lists are relatively short compared with the long lists of problems menopause can trigger.

The good news about side effects is they are usually temporary. Once your body has a few weeks or months to adjust to the increased hormone levels, things generally stabilize.

If you are among the group of women who take hormone therapy only to relieve the symptoms of menopause, you can use it for a relatively short time—say a year or two. If you have a family history of osteoporosis or heart disease, you'll want to take the hormones for at least 10 years, possibly even longer. Current research shows that the longer you take hormones, the better off you are.

WHAT IF YOU WANT TO STOP?

If you decide to stop HRT, talk to your doctor first! Then follow his or her guidelines, which probably will include the following:

- DON'T stop "cold turkey!" Taper off gradually.

- Start by taking your HRT every other day, then take it twice a week, then once a week, then stop. This process should take a month or two.

- Remember that the same symptoms you took the HRT for in the first place can resurface if you should suddenly decide to just stop the therapy.

WHAT CHOICES DO YOU HAVE?

Hormone replacement therapy is big business, no question about it. At this time, conventional HRT costs about a dollar per day. A table listing some suppliers and products currently available is included on page 142. Because new products are introduced every few months, be sure to check with your doctor about your current options.

What's EPART?

(Estrogen-Progestogen-Androgen Replacement Therapy)

Androgen is a male hormone, a form of testosterone. Research has shown that a small, but apparently significant, amount of this hormone is produced in the ovaries of menstruating women. At menopause, the levels decrease significantly. The result is what we call "lost lust syndrome."

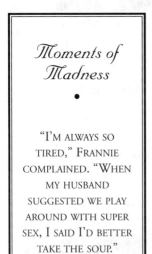

Moments of Madness

•

"I'M ALWAYS SO TIRED," FRANNIE COMPLAINED. "WHEN MY HUSBAND SUGGESTED WE PLAY AROUND WITH SUPER SEX, I SAID I'D BETTER TAKE THE SOUP."

The lack of testosterone may make you lose interest in sex. If this happens and you want to change it, talk to your doctor about low-dose testosterone. This lack of sexual desire is particularly common after surgical menopause with removal of the ovaries.

More about the types of hormone replacement

Hormones can be delivered to your body in several different forms. No single delivery system is right for everybody, but each system has an advantage.

Pills are convenient for many women, but they can cause problems for other women. When swallowed, the hormones pass through the liver before they are absorbed into the bloodstream. If you have liver damage or a history of liver disease, you and your doctor will want to consider alternatives. In addition, some doctors believe oral therapy can lead to an increase in gallbladder disease. So if gallstones are a possibility for you, you may want to think about another delivery mode.

Alternatives to pills are intramuscular injections (shots) or, if you have needle phobia, transdermal patches. The patch slowly releases a steady amount of estrogen over a specific number of days. Then you put on a new patch.

Another method uses a pellet of hormone implanted beneath the skin. The hormone is absorbed slowly over several months. There are some disadvantages to this method, and it is not very popular in the United States.

Nightly vaginal creams are prescribed mostly to overcome vaginal dryness. At first, you use it every other day. Once the dryness improves, the cream can be used less often—once every five to seven days or so to keep these sensitive tissues healthy.

Many European women use a hormone cream that is spread on the lower abdomen. Unfortunately, this cream is not yet available in the United States. Watch for more information about this.

In light of all these alternatives, you and your doctor will want to discuss which delivery method is right for you.

WHAT IF YOU CAN'T TAKE HORMONES?

If you and your doctor decide that hormone replacement therapy is not an option for you, you'll want to discuss other ways to relieve your symptoms. If you can't take estrogen, perhaps you can take progesterone. This can be effective in helping to decrease the frequency and severity of hot flashes and other symptoms.

Tranquilizers have been used by some women. Valium®, for example, suppresses hypothalamic function and can relieve symptoms. This is not to be used for too long, however, since it can be addictive, and you can build up a tolerance to it.

Sedatives, which decrease autonomic nervous system irritability, are sometimes prescribed. However, they should be used with extreme caution, since they are also habit-forming and can be potentially dangerous.

Clonidine®, a medicine usually prescribed for hypertension, sometimes relieves hot flashes. A less effective drug option is Bellergal®, an antispasmodic drug that sometimes helps hot flashes. This one should be tried only if everything else fails.

Also worthy of mention are Rejuvex® and Femtrol®. Both are over-the-counter products designed to be taken as food supplements. Rejuvex® contains raw glandular powders from cows. Femtrol® contains dong quai, an herb used by women in China for thousands of years, plus other herbs recognized as having "estrogenic" properties. Recent information also suggests supplemental boron, the antioxidant vitamins, and selenium could be helpful. These are often recommended by alternative medicine specialists.

Many of today's alternative formulas are based on plants identified as having "phytoestrogens" as part of their chemical composition. Dong quai, licorice, and black cohosh all contain phytoestrogens. Phytoestrogens are believed to mediate the effects of estrogen. That is, when you are low, they supplement; when you have too much, they neutralize. More study is needed to clarify exactly how these plants affect the body.

Here are some of the nutritional supplements you may want to consider during the perimenopausal years if you cannot take hormones.

—Vitamin E for relief of hot flashes and leg cramps

—Vitamin B complex for stress

—Vitamin C to relieve general symptoms

—Calcium for bone health and to promote sleep

You may have heard about the root valerian, often sold in health food stores. This is a powerful plant sedative used through the ages by women with painful menstrual cramps. It is said to promote sleep, relieve headaches, decrease anxiety, and reduce fatigue. However, it can be habit-forming if used too often. Valerian should never be used if you are already taking an antidepressant because the combination can cause serious side effects.

Another folk remedy sometimes recommended is ginseng, a root that contains natural estrogen. If you cannot take estrogen, it is not wise to use ginseng, either. Even if you can take estrogen, most women should take it with progesterone. Excessive amounts of ginseng can have the same effect as unopposed estrogen, causing an increase in growth of the uterine lining. One of the major drawbacks with ginseng is that you never know exactly how much estrogen you're getting, so you may endanger your health.

Moments of Madness

•

"FUNNY THING," SARAH ANNOUNCED AT OUR HOT FLASHERS' LUNCH. "WHEN I COMPLAINED TO MY DOCTOR ABOUT MEMORY LOSS, HE MADE ME PAY IN ADVANCE."

If you want more information, the National Institute of Health recently opened an office in Washington D.C. for the study of alternative therapies. Contact the NIH to see if they have information on your particular area of interest.

A very important consideration if you can't take estrogen, and even if you can, is to watch your diet. It needs to be well balanced and contain at least 1200 to 1800 calories daily to meet the changing needs of your body. If you need to watch your weight, increase your exercise, but don't scrimp on calories or overdose on protein and completely cut out fat. Your body has basic nutritional needs, and these are heightened by the stresses of menopause. (See Chapter 6 for more information.)

Other nonconventional therapies include acupuncture, said to relieve hot flashes and headaches; yoga exercises, which emphasize breathing, calmness, and focusing your attention on stretches that benefit your circulation and keep you supple; homeopathics, some of which are mentioned above; and meditation.

SUPPORTING YOUR BODY

Even with hormone replacement, there are some things you'll want to do to assure your body of adequate support during the perimenopausal years. For example, a good multivitamin with minerals may be helpful, along with a diet rich in calcium, vitamin E, and the B complex vitamins.

Also, both the adrenal system and the liver work overtime during the perimenopausal years. Anything you can do to "support" these organs can help your body. Specifically, you can cut back on sugar, alcohol, and caffeine and increase your intake of whole grains, beans, and legumes.

Here's another tip. Remember good old oatmeal, the kind your mother made years ago? Well, it's proving to be a wonder food for perimenopausal women. Among oatmeal's many virtues are its role in:

—Reducing cholesterol and risk of heart disease

—Improving circulation

—Nourishing your nervous system

—Reducing headaches

—Easing bladder problems and vaginal dryness

—Promoting good restful sleep

—Building strong bones

—Maintaining healthy teeth

—Stabilizing blood sugar levels

—Relieving depression and mood swings

That list might just tempt you to go back to a breakfast of good old oatmeal once or twice a week. Even if these benefits are exaggerated, a little oatmeal can't hurt.

WHAT DOES HORMONE THERAPY COST?

The current estimate is that hormone replacement therapy has the potential for *saving* $3.5 billion each year in medical costs for American women.

This estimate looks at the cost of hormone therapy (which in 1995 was about $1 per woman per day), plus the cost of regular physical examinations. These expenses were then compared with the amount of money spent for treating osteoporosis, arteriosclerotic heart disease, and the other disorders linked with hormone deficiency.

Supplier	Brand Name	Hormone	Generic Name
Abbott	Ogen Ogen Vaginal Cream	Oral estrogen Estrogen vaginal cream	Estropipate Estropipate
Bristol Myers	Megace	Progestin	Megesterol acetate
Carnick Amen		Progestin	Medroxprogesterone acetate
Ciba-Geigy	Estraderm	Estrogen (patch)	Transdermal
ICN Pharm.	Android/Testred/Oreton	Androgen	Methyl testosterone
Lilly	Diethylstilbestrol Suppositories	Estrogen vaginal cream	Diethylstilbestrol
Mead Johnson	Estrace Estrace Vaginal Cream	Oral estrogen Estrogen vaginal cream	Micronized estrad ol 17 beta-estradiol
Merrill-Dow	Tace	Oral estrogen	Chlorotrianisene
Ortho	Ortho Dienestrol Cream Micronor	Estrogen vaginal cream Progestin	Dienestrol Norethindrone
Park-Davis	Estovis Norlutate Norlutin	Oral estrogen Progestin Progesterone	Quinestrol Norethindrone acetate Norethindrone

Schering	Estinyl	Oral estrogen	Ethinyl estradiol
Solvay	Estratab	Oral estrogen	Esterified estrogen
	Estregard Cream	Estrogen vaginal cream	Dienestrol
	Estraval intramuscular (IM)	parenteral estrogen	Valerate
	Curretabs	Progestin	Medroxyprogesterone acetate
	Estratest	Estrogen/androgen	Esterified estrogens + methyl testosterone
Squibb	Delestrogen (IM)	Parenteral estrogen	Estradiol valerate
Syntex	Nor-Q.D.	Progestin	Norethindrone
Upjohn	Depo-Estradiol (IM)	Parenteral estrogen	Estradiol cypionate
	Provera	Progestin	Medroxyprogesterone acetate
	Depo-Testadiol (inject.)	Estrogen/androgen	Estradiol cypionate + testosterone cypionate
Wyeth-Ayerst	Premarin	Oral estrogen	Conjugated estrogens
	Premarin Vaginal Cream	Estrogen vaginal cream	Conjugated estrogens
	Premarin (IM, IV)	Parenteral estrogen	Conjugated estrogens
	Cycrin	Progestin	Medroxyprogesterone acetate
	Aygestin	Progestin	Norethindrone acetate
	Ovrette	Progestin	Norgestrol
	Premarin + methyl testosterone	Estrogen/androgen	Conjugated estrogen + methyl testosterone

*H*YSTERECTOMY: WHY AND WHEN?

*S*usan and Sally are identical twins. Born and raised in a mid-sized midwestern city, both girls were athletic, healthy, and strong. When they were teenagers, their taste in boyfriends never conflicted, and they both married their high school beaus.

After a struggle to put their husbands through college, the women returned to school before starting their families. Susan had her first child when she was 29; Sally had hers at 30. Susan had another child when she turned 32. Sally had her second son at age 33. Life was wonderful for the women, raising their families in stable marriages. It was nearly idyllic. Like many twins, these women remained close throughout most of their lives.

Career moves and eventual retirement caused Sally and Susan to move to opposite corners of the world. Susan and her husband, Bob, moved to Honolulu. Sally and Doug ended up in Florida.

Susan and Sally both began to notice perimenopausal changes around age 47. Menopause finally occurred for Susan at age 54. Sally stopped menstruating altogether when she was 55. They each experienced a few hot flashes, memory lapses, and mood swings, but, all in all, menopause was not difficult for them.

Susan and Sally both had a history of fibroids, which their doctors watched and which never really bothered them much. When Susan went for her annual checkup after her final period, her doctor in Honolulu noted that there was a fibroid "about the size of a grapefruit." Susan said, "That's strange. I haven't really been bothered by it. What do you think I should do?" The doctor then discussed the pros and cons of hormone replacement with Susan and told her the best course of action was for her to study the facts about HRT and together they would watch the fibroid. "For now," the doctor told her, "I think it's best to do nothing."

The next time Susan talked to Sally, she learned that Sally, too, had been diagnosed with a fibroid about the size of a grapefruit. But Sally's doctor had been adamant about Sally's need to have the fibroid, her uterus, cervix, tubes, and ovaries taken out as soon as possible. The doctor led Sally to believe this surgery was urgent.

After they talked, both women went for second opinions. Susan's consulting gynecologist concurred with her own doctor. The best course of action, whether she decided on hormone replacement therapy or not, was the conservative "wait and see" approach.

Sally's consulting doctor likewise agreed with her own gynecologist, and she went ahead with the surgery. She began estrogen replacement therapy while she was in the hospital. In the meantime, Susan had begun hormone replacement therapy, too, deciding that the risks she faced in the potential for the increase in fibroid growth and uterine cancer were less serious to her well-being than the risks for osteoporosis and heart disease. She felt she still had a lot of tennis games to play, and she didn't want to lose any more bone mass than she possibly already had.

It took Sally almost six months to begin to feel like doing anything again. She felt completely exhausted after her surgery, even with the estrogen. She pretty much lost interest in her husband, and it seemed sex was a thing of the past. She became very angry when she looked at Susan, who had not had surgery but who still had a large fibroid. The fibroid just wasn't a problem for her.

"It's funny," Sally said, "I really wasn't that bothered by my fibroid either. I wonder why my doctor recommended surgery. It seems *like Susan is doing so much better than I am. She's going on full power just like I used to do, but I just can't anymore."*

Susan never did have surgery for her fibroid. It shrunk slightly, then stabilized. Her course of estrogen balanced by progestogens worked well for her. The two women were quite bewildered at how this situation turned out. The sister who "took the cure" fared poorly, while the untreated sister thrived.

Hysterectomy. The very word should give us pause. As a medical procedure, hysterectomy was first recorded in Greece about 1700 years ago. It was the Egyptians, however, who associated the uterus with the puzzling physical and emotional complaints now referred to as hysteria.

The Egyptians believed that the uterus migrated inside the female body and that its displacement caused strange behaviors. They used exotic herbal preparations: some were to smell; some to eat, and others to place between a woman's legs in hopes that the migrant uterus would return to its proper position.

The first subtotal hysterectomy was performed in 1843 for an enlarged uterus. In 1850, a doctor named Burnham performed the first total abdominal hysterectomy. Mortality and morbidity for hysterectomy remained high for decades. With the advent of antibiotics and the development of more sophisticated surgical techniques and instruments, mortality and morbidity with hysterectomy have declined continuously since about 1890.

So far this decade, more than 650,000 hysterectomies are being done each year in the United States alone. The U.S.

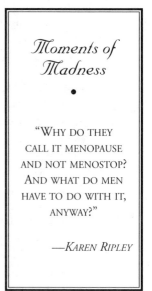

Moments of Madness

•

"WHY DO THEY CALL IT MENOPAUSE AND NOT MENOSTOP? AND WHAT DO MEN HAVE TO DO WITH IT, ANYWAY?"

—*KAREN RIPLEY*

Bureau of the Census predicts the number will hit 824,000 by 2005. This makes hysterectomy the second most frequently performed major surgery. (The first is Caesarean section.) It also means that more than 12 million American women have had hysterectomies in the last 10 years, and that one in three women is likely to have one before she reaches age 65.

Curiously, there are marked differences in hysterectomy rates from country to country and from region to region within the U.S. The highest hysterectomy rate in the United States has occurred consistently in the South. There the rate has been two and a half times higher than the rate for the Northeast, which has consistently been the lowest.

For Sally, it's possible that surgery was recommended because Southerners tend to believe that the woman's reproductive system has little or no value except in reproduction. Once the need for reproduction ends, the system can and should be removed. For Susan, out in Hawaii, the prevailing attitude toward reproductive systems might be just the opposite. There the doctors might consider that there are continuing benefits from retaining the uterus and ovaries that outweigh minor discomforts caused by fibroids.

Many women wonder if they will experience menopause after hysterectomy. The answer depends on exactly what organs are removed at hysterectomy. The term has become a kind of generic one that refers to general removal of the female organs. But we need to be precise these days. Perhaps we even need to do away with the term hysterectomy and end once and for all its association with hysteria.

In general, the term hysterectomy refers to the removal of the uterus. After a hysterectomy, a woman will no longer menstruate. But she will continue to ovulate. Thus, removing the uterus alone does not cause menopause. If the ovaries are left intact, they continue to produce eggs and release hormones until natural menopause. Unless hysterectomy has been accompanied by what is termed bilateral oophorectomy, you should still have your ovaries.

There are actually three types of hysterectomy surgery:

>   —Total or complete hysterectomy, in which the
>   body of the uterus and the cervix are removed;

>   —Radical hysterectomy, performed for certain
>   cancers of the reproductive organs, in which the
>   uterus, cervix, supporting ligaments and tissues,
>   the upper portion of the vagina, and the pelvic
>   lymph nodes may all be removed. (Whenever the
>   word "radical" is included, cancer is usually
>   involved.)

>   —Subtotal, partial, or supracervical hysterectomy,
>   in which the uterus is removed, but not the cervix.

When the fallopian tubes and the ovaries are removed with the uterus, the procedure is referred to as a total hysterectomy with bilateral salpingo-oophorectomy (meaning both ovaries are removed with the fallopian tubes). In some cases, only one ovary is removed. That procedure is called a unilateral oophorectomy.

The National Center for Health Statistics reports that about 45% of all hysterectomies performed include removal of both ovaries. If you are not sure what organs were removed at the time of your hysterectomy, check your medical records to find out. More precisely, ask to read the operative and the pathology reports.

When the ovaries are removed, some women experience what has become known as "surgical menopause." Symptoms common to menopause, including hot flashes, vaginal dryness, night sweats, and dizziness, among others, can be sudden and severe.

Hormone replacement therapy started immediately after bilateral oophorectomy can help alleviate these symptoms, but because the exact dosage for each woman varies, some symptoms can recur until the right amounts of the various hormones are determined.

If your ovaries were removed at hysterectomy, chances are you'd know it, even if you began hormone replacement therapy right away. If only one ovary was removed, your body will still be able to produce some estrogen, and menopause is likely to occur at its natural time.

HOW ARE HYSTERECTOMIES PERFORMED?

With a vaginal hysterectomy, the uterus is removed through the vagina. This procedure requires no abdominal incision. Many women report less pain and seem to recover quicker than with abdominal hysterectomy. This procedure, however, does carry some risk of postoperative infection. Because hospital stays are shorter, this alternative is a bit more cost-effective than abdominal hysterectomy.

Abdominal hysterectomy is done through an incision in the abdomen. This procedure is used about 70 to 80 percent of the time. It is often used for cancer, endometriosis, large fibroids, or chronic infections of the fallopian tubes, ovaries, or uterus.

This procedure requires a longer hospital stay than the vaginal approach, and women who have abdominal hysterectomy are more likely to require blood transfusions. Costs are higher than those with vaginal hysterectomy.

Laparoscopically assisted vaginal hysterectomy (LAVH) is also done under general anesthesia. The surgeon makes some tiny incisions (only about one centimeter long) in the abdomen. A miniature camera connected to the special viewing instrument (laparoscope) projects a magnified image of the internal organs onto a video monitor. Other instruments inserted through the same incisions can then be used to remove the organs and seal the cut tissue. Instead of facing a long recovery period, women who have LAVH can usually return to full activity in less than a week. The disadvantage with this procedure is the cost.

WHO NEEDS A HYSTERECTOMY?

Many women wonder about the overwhelming frequency of hysterectomy. In some cases, a hysterectomy may be life-saving. In younger women who have severe uterine bleeding after childbirth or those with severe infections, hysterectomy may be the only available option. Also, when invasive cancer is present in the cervix, uterus, fallopian tubes, or ovaries, hysterectomy may be recommended. Further, hysterectomy may be useful in managing colon, rectum, or bladder cancers.

There are other conditions for which hysterectomy is often recommended, but for which there may be other alternatives. The chronic pain and heavy bleeding associated with fibroids, endometriosis, and other disorders do not necessarily dictate hysterectomy, even though it may be and usually is suggested as a best course of action. Likewise, genital prolapse, which can cause bladder and bowel control problems, once was considered a clear indication for hysterectomy. Today there are other options.

WHAT ABOUT FIBROIDS?

Fibroids are balls of muscular tissue that grow inside the lining of the uterus, on the outer surface of the uterus, or within the muscular uterine wall. They are also known as leiomyomas. Thirty percent of all hysterectomies are done because of fibroids, which are rarely cancerous.

The incidence of fibroids is quite high. One of every four women over the age of 35 is believed to have fibroids. Also, the incidence tends to be higher in African-American women than other women. Half of the women with fibroids never have any symptoms and need no treatment at all.

Fibroids may be found in a variety of locations. Subserous fibroids protrude from the surface of the uterus into the pelvic cavity. Intramural fibroids are located deep inside the uterine wall, and submucosal fibroids extend from the endometrial lining into the uterine cavity.

The growth of many fibroids may be dependent on estrogen, while others lack estrogen receptors and do not grow because of estrogen. Fibroids may get bigger during pregnancy and shrink at menopause when estrogen decreases. Even if they are small, fibroids can be troublesome for some women, however, causing heavy or prolonged menstrual bleeding. When fibroids are large, they can cause urinary frequency, pelvic heaviness, and discomfort.

Treating fibroids

One option for managing fibroids is simply keeping an eye on them. They should be evaluated periodically for growth and discomfort. Pelvic examination, ultrasound, and laparoscopy may all be used.

A new drug category, although not yet approved by the FDA to treat fibroids, is gonadotropin-releasing-hormone agonists. These block estrogen production and thus cause fibroids to shrink. However, the drugs can trigger menopausal symptoms and so are usually used for short-term treatment. Once the drugs are discontinued, the fibroids tend to grow back to their original size within several months. For that reason, drug therapy may prove most useful for shrinking the fibroids before surgery, which can make the procedure more comfortable.

Another surgical treatment for fibroids is called myomectomy. In this procedure, fibroids are cut out of the uterus and removed through a conventional incision in the abdomen or by laparoscopic or hysteroscopic techniques. Once reserved for women who wanted to retain their child-bearing capacity, myomectomy preserves the uterus and cervix. Today there is some evidence that preserving the uterus and cervix beyond menopause may be important not only for preserving urogenital and sexual functions, but also for future cardiovascular health.

Myomectomy is often more complicated than hysterectomy, and there are serious risks associated with it. It can take as long or even longer than a hysterectomy, may cause more blood loss, and carries a long recovery time—four to six weeks. The principal difficulty with myomectomy, and probably the reason why it is primarily used for women under age 40, is that it does not prevent fibroids from growing back. This means more surgery may be required, and eventually hysterectomy may be needed anyway.

WHAT IS ENDOMETRIOSIS?

Endometriosis is a disorder in which endometrial tissue, which normally lines the uterus, grows in other parts of the body. Most often it is found in the pelvic area, but it has been reported elsewhere, sometimes far afield. Displaced endometrial tissue thickens and bleeds, much like the lining of the uterus, but it is not expelled during menstruation. Instead it may continue to cause inflammation and the formation of scar tissue, sometimes accompanied by severe pain.

Treating endometriosis

The less uncomfortable symptoms of endometriosis can be treated with pain medication and anti-inflammatory drugs. Moderate exercise and birth control pills also can help to relieve heavy bleeding, but regular checkups to monitor the condition are extremely important. There is some evidence that endometriosis, like fibroids, is related to estrogen production.

Among the surgical treatments for endometriosis are electro-coagulation, in which tissue is burned away; excision, in which tissue is cut out using a scalpel; and laparoscopically assisted laser surgery. High-precision lasers can destroy endometrial growths on the ovaries, fallopian tubes, and uterus without damaging the organs themselves. This is believed to be an advantage over the scalpel or electrocautery, but it is very costly. These are all considered conservative approaches to endometriosis and are especially helpful when a woman wants to preserve fertility.

Since estrogen may make endometriosis worse, you must bring this condition to your doctor's attention before you start hormone replacement therapy. As estrogen production wanes, endometriosis, like fibroids, diminishes. If you are not incapacitated by pain, doing nothing is an acceptable course of action. More often than not, however, endometriosis causes serious discomfort, and you'll want to discuss all of the options, including laparoscopically assisted laser surgery and hysterectomy, with your doctor.

DYSFUNCTIONAL UTERINE BLEEDING

About 20% of all hysterectomies performed are because of abnormal or "dysfunctional" uterine bleeding. If you are past menopause, remember that any bleeding is considered abnormal and requires immediate medical attention.

Before menopause, some women have bleeding that is severely incapacitating. Also, this type of heavy bleeding can lead to anemia and can disrupt lifestyle.

What to do about bleeding

The first step, of course, is to consult a gynecologist to rule out pregnancy, tumor, or infection and to find the cause of the bleeding. Progesterone alone can often stop the bleeding, which is sometimes caused by a simple overgrowth of the uterine lining as hormone levels fluctuate. In more complicated cases, anti-inflammatory drugs, oral contraceptive pills, or hormone replacement therapy sometimes helps.

Dilation and curettage (D & C), in which the cervix is dilated and the linings of the cervical canal and the uterus are scraped with a small spoon-shaped instrument, is another potentially effective approach.

THE ROLE OF ENDOMETRIAL ABLATION

A relatively new procedure, endometrial ablation, is another alternative to hysterectomy for uterine bleeding of unknown cause that has not responded to simpler treatments.

In this procedure, the patient is given general, spinal, or local anesthesia. The doctor views the inside of the uterus through a hysteroscope to identify the endometrial area. Then "electrodessication" or "photovaporization" is used to destroy the unhealthy tissue. Defining the differences between these two approaches is beyond the scope of this book, but both do the job effectively. If you want more information about exactly how the procedure will be done, don't hesitate to ask your doctor. You have a right to understand what is happening.

Hysteroscopic endometrial ablation is associated with less risk of infection, shorter hospitalization, and lower cost than hysterectomy. There are, however, some potential complications, including bleeding and injuries to adjacent organs. In most cases, however, the procedure is considered very safe.

Some studies have shown that use of hormones before ablation improves the outcome for some women. In others, suction curettage before ablation helps. Discuss all these possible approaches with your doctor and get as much information as you can before you make your decision.

It is possible that bleeding can recur after any or all of these procedures. If that is the case, you may consider a second endometrial ablation or a hysterectomy.

GENITAL OR UTERINE PROLAPSE

When the ligaments that support the pelvic organs weaken, genital or uterine prolapse can occur. The pelvic organs begin to sag, sometimes causing pressure, urinary incontinence, or rectal discomfort. Prolapse can result from age, from estrogen deficiency, from obesity, or from pregnancies that have stretched and weakened the pelvic floor and its supporting muscles.

In the past, hysterectomy was considered the best treatment for prolapse-related urinary incontinence. About 15 percent of all hysterectomies are done to correct prolapse. But other options are also available.

Other options for treating prolapse

• *The pessary*

A pessary is a diaphragm-like device that can be inserted into the vagina to support the uterus and treat prolapse-related urinary incontinence. By supporting the uterus, pressure on the bladder can be reduced, relieving incontinence and discomfort.

Pessaries tend to be most effective when they are used along with estrogen. When estrogen is not an option and the vagina is dry, pessaries can cause vaginal erosion with bleeding.

Estrogen, as either a vaginal cream or an oral medication, improves the collagen content of the support tissue in the pelvic area. Some combination of creams and oral medication may give the best results.

When conservative treatments fail and surgery is inconvenient, the pessary can give temporary relief. If serious illness or a history of surgeries make further surgical repair impossible, a pessary may be the best option.

Some women abandon the pessary after a time if they experience ulceration or if prolapse gets worse. For these women, reconstructive surgery may be in order.

• *Reconstructive surgery*

A "resuspension" procedure can sometimes be done to pull the organs back up to their proper positions. With this operation, the ligaments supporting the pelvic organs are shored up to correct the prolapse. Another procedure, which uses collagen injections, also offers promise. Discuss these options with your gynecologist. Then get a list of surgeons who have performed these procedures in your community.

• *Kegel exercises*

Kegel exercises to strengthen the muscles in the pelvic region can also be useful. These exercises are described in Chapter 2 (page 96) and should be practiced daily to increase the support structure for the pelvic organs.

• *Estrogen replacement therapy in prolapse*

Estrogen creams or oral estrogen improves the collagen content of the ligaments that support the pelvic area. This is the most convenient treatment and is often the first thing doctors will try.

If all else fails . . .

If all these options fail, hysterectomy may be in order. Be sure to ask your doctor for exact information about how the procedure will be done and what you should expect afterward.

OTHER REASONS FOR HYSTERECTOMY

Hysterectomy may be recommended because of specific medical conditions, including chronic pelvic pain of unknown origin, pelvic adhesions, and pelvic inflammatory disease. All of these are serious and require careful medical management. Your physician, acting as your partner in managing your health, is often your best guide to handling the symptoms of these disorders.

Why not just have a hysterectomy and be done with it? New findings provide some good reasons for retaining your uterus throughout your lifetime. It was once thought (and many gynecologists still believe) that the uterus had only one function—supporting a pregnancy. However, the respected Framingham Heart Study found that premenopausal women who had hysterectomies had a three-times greater risk of heart attack than their counterparts who had retained the uterus.

We now know that the uterus produces prostacyclin, the most potent known inhibitor of blood clots, and may, thus, offer protection from strokes and heart attacks. When the uterus is removed, that protection is reduced or disappears.

Beyond its responses to estrogen, the uterus is the center of complex interactions involving other prostaglandins and prostacyclins, which increase vaginal tone and change the shape of the uterus at orgasm. Therefore, sexual satisfaction may be affected when the uterus is removed. Recent evidence suggests that the cervix, too, may play a role in sexual satisfaction, contrary to long-held beliefs.

In addition, if the ovaries are removed at hysterectomy, premenopausal women who cannot take replacement hormones face increased long-term risks, including osteoporosis and other disorders, in addition to cardiovascular disease.

Finally, hysterectomy is a very serious operation. In the United States, 600 women die each year because of complications of hysterectomy.

BEFORE YOU SAY YES TO HYSTERECTOMY

You have a right to know everything there is to know about any procedure before you agree to have it. Be sure you ask the two most basic questions:

(1) Do I really need it?

(2) Will it take care of my problem?

Dr. Barbara Levy, working with the National Women's Health Resource Center, has developed a list of questions that women may want to ask when their doctors have recommended hysterectomy.

While these questions go beyond what is referred to as the "BRAIDED" concept of informed consent in vogue in the early 1990s, you may want to take the lead and get as much information as is available. (This "BRAIDED" medical concept stands for Benefits, Risk, Alternatives, Information, Decision, Education, and Documentation.)

1. What problem are you trying to treat?

2. What are all the methods available to treat this problem?

3. Why are you recommending one medical approach over others to treat my condition?

4. What is the worst that can happen if I decide not to follow this recommendation?

5. What can I expect following surgery? What will be the same? What will be different?

6. What reading material can you recommend to help me learn more about this treatment option, as well as about other options?

7. Can you recommend a specialist for a second opinion? *(Note:* Many insurance companies require a second opinion before surgery. Beyond that it is valuable to get a second opinion to help build confidence in your surgeon. If the second opinion is different from the first, go for a third. Network with other women to find doctors with experience in treating your particular condition.)

8. How many of the recommended procedures have you performed? What specialized or advanced training is required to perform this procedure?

9. What are the success and failure rates of this procedure?

10. What complications are possible with this procedure?

11. Can you recommend former patients who had this procedure who might be willing to talk to me about their experiences? (While patient information is confidential, your doctor may have a list of women interested in helping other women make their decisions.)

The Psychological Side

According to a recent report from the National Women's Health Resource Center, women need to be aware of the emotional and psychological aspects of hysterectomy. While emotional responses vary from woman to woman, identifying feelings commonly connected with hysterectomy is an important part of the decision-making process. Being aware of these feelings is very important to your successful recovery after surgery.

Feelings identified with hysterectomy include:

—A sense of loss, for both body parts (uterus and ovaries) and function (fertility)

—Sadness, anger, depression, and/or anxiety in response to the loss

—A diminished sense of femininity, attractiveness, or self-worth

—Anxiety about sexuality

Before surgery, it is important to discuss your feelings and your expectations with your partner and your friends. Get as much information as possible before the procedure to help you feel in control. Evaluate your personal responses to each of the feelings. How do you handle depression? What about anger? Talk about this with your support group, friends, or family. Consider what your reproductive organs symbolize for you. Be realistic about what to expect after the surgery.

If you need to find a support group to help you handle this decision, talk to your doctor. Some hospitals have social workers who can help, and if there is a women's health center in your area, there may be a hysterectomy support group. At the end of this chapter, we've included a list of places to contact for more information.

It is clear that for thousands of women, hysterectomy is life-saving and/or improves the quality of life. But for a significant group of other women, in addition to the emotional and psychological considerations, there are physical sequelae. The Center for Health Statistics reports that 25 to 30 percent of all hysterectomy patients may experience one or more complications from the surgery. These include:

- Fever and infection after surgery

- Urinary tract infections or discomfort

- Sudden hormonal decreases (with symptoms of menopause)

- Constipation

- Fatigue or decreased energy

- Depression

- Pain or discomfort during intercourse

- Loss of sexual pleasure or interest

And the more serious possible complications:

- Hemorrhage requiring transfusion

- Injury to the bowel or bladder during surgery, requiring repair

- Life-threatening cardiopulmonary problems

In about 25 percent of women, hysterectomy affects estrogen production even when an ovary is preserved. Many cases of premature ovarian failure occur because the ovarian blood supply is interrupted. The uterine artery may supply part of the blood to the ovaries, and if it is removed with the uterus, the ovaries may stop working. Be aware of how your body is responding after surgery, and be sure to discuss hormone replacement therapy with your doctor.

WHAT HAPPENS AFTER SURGERY?

After hysterectomy, doctors usually prescribe estrogen alone. Physicians have long believed that progesterones are only useful for preventing endometrial or uterine cancer. Once the uterus is removed, they believe there is no need for the protection afforded by progesterones.

Even though women don't need to worry about uterine cancer once the uterus is removed, progesterone deficiency can still cause uncomfortable symptoms.

The balance between progesterone and estrogen protects against premenstrual syndrome (PMS), breast cancer, osteoporosis, cardiovascular disease, and hot flashes, flushing, and other symptoms. Estrogen and progesterone work together throughout a woman's reproductive life to maintain emotional and physical balance. These two hormones have also been shown to directly affect the neurotransmitters that regulate mood, appetite, sleep, and pain perception.

When progesterone production declines, some women may experience PMS for the first time in their lives. Treatment with natural progesterones will often alleviate these symptoms and restore balance.

Dr. John R. Lee, author of *Natural Progesterone: The Multiple Roles of a Remarkable Hormone,* writes that breast cancer is more likely to occur in premenopausal women with normal or high estrogen levels and low progesterone levels. This imbalance tends to be fairly common after about age 35, when periods of anovulation begin to occur. This same situation occurs in menopausal women who are not given progesterone.

Dr. Lee reported that the cancer protection afforded by progesterone is clear. His prospective study showed premenopausal women with low progesterone levels had 5.4 times the risk of developing breast cancer and a 10-fold increase in deaths from all malignant neoplasms compared with those with normal progesterone levels.

Progesterone was also found to play a role in protecting women from heart attack and in maintaining bone mass and slowing the bone deterioration from osteoporosis. There is current research underway to learn more, but these preliminary results suggest that full hormone replacement therapy that includes both progesterone and estrogen may be best after hysterectomy.

What about the risks? When dosage levels are properly monitored and balanced (that balance may be different for each woman), hormone therapy does not appear to increase the risk for cancer. In fact, with the addition of progesterone, the risk may actually decrease.

Progesterone is thought to be particularly important for women with a family history of cardiovascular disease or osteoporosis. However, the improved quality of emotional and physical health is the most noticeable benefit of progesterone therapy. If hysterectomy is the best option for your particular problem, ask your doctor about the benefits of taking progesterone along with estrogen.

Does your sex drive die after hysterectomy?

Some—but certainly not all—women seem to lose interest in sex after hysterectomy. While their doctors might insist that this is part of the postsurgical depression and that hormone replacement therapy will correct the problem with time, not everyone agrees.

Some studies suggest that when the ovaries are removed or stop working, an important source of testosterone (responsible for the sex drive) also is lost. Although the testosterone disappears gradually with natural menopause, surgical menopause produces a sudden drop.

One of the few studies to look at this problem showed that sexual thoughts and coitus decreased to a greater extent with a drop in testosterone levels than with reductions in estrogen. A Canadian study found that women who received an estrogen-androgen preparation (testosterone is an androgen) showed a four- to six-fold increase in the frequency of coitus and orgasm, compared with women who did not receive androgen. Androgens cause some side effects, however, including liver problems, acne, edema, vaginal keratosis, and changes in texture or amount of body hair. For some women, the loss of libido may be preferred.

WHAT'S THE BOTTOM LINE?

In the final analysis, the literature suggests that about half of all hysterectomies performed today may be unnecessary. The procedure is serious, costly, and has long-term implications for women's health.

Dr. Francis L. Hutchins, Jr., director of gynecology and women's services at the Graduate Hospital in Philadelphia, said:

"Curing a pelvic disease with a hysterectomy is the equivalent of treating a mild headache with decapitation. Treat the disease, don't get rid of the organ."

Women have an important role to play in changing doctors' perceptions that the uterus is only important during a woman's reproductive years. By becoming informed, and by getting second and even third opinions when hysterectomy is recommended, a new dialogue on the subject can begin. Only when women start to take greater control over their bodies and what happens to them will we begin to see a reduction in the number of unnecessary hysterectomies.

FOR MORE INFORMATION

—American College of Obstetricians and Gynecologists (ACOG), 403 12th St. SW, Washington, DC 20024

The ACOG has published a pamphlet titled "Understanding Hysterectomy," which outlines what constitutes a medically necessary hysterectomy and describes what the surgery involves.

—National Women's Health Resource Center, 2440 M Street, N.W., #325, Washington, DC 20037

For $15 ($10 to members), the Center provides comprehensive information about hysterectomy and the conditions leading to hysterectomy.

—HERS Foundation (Hysterectomy Educational Resource and Services), Nora Coffey, President, 422 Bryn Mawr Avenue, Bala Cynwyd, PA 19004

This foundation provides personal counseling, information, and answers to specific questions on the alternatives to hysterectomy and the consequences of the surgery. Call (215) 667-7757 between 9 a.m. and 5 p.m. (Eastern time zone).

—Endometriosis Association, PO Box 92187, Milwaukee, WI 53202

If you have been diagnosed with endometriosis, you may want to consider joining this organization. Contact them at (414) 962-8972 for literature and support group information.

—The Institute for Reproductive Health, 8721 Beverly Boulevard, Los Angeles, CA 90048

This institute maintains a resource library on women's health care issues, provides specific information, and sponsors support groups. Write or call (213) 854-6375 for more information.

CHAPTER V

ℒIVING HEALTHFULLY EVER AFTER

𝒮ome lucky women (no one has yet estimated how many), cruise through the menopausal years with little or no discomfort. One day their periods stop, and they just go about their business, not noticing any dramatic changes in their health or their lives. But surviving menopause is not an end unto itself. It's another step up the ladder of life, but the goal isn't just life. It's life with vigor, excitement, and quality. To assure that the next 30 to 50 years are as good or even better than the first 50, you'll want to have a team of health specialists to help you.

PICKING A HEALTH CARE TEAM

If you're coping with a chronic illness, you probably already have a front-line physician on your team. As we age, we need to add others. For women, the gynecologist is particularly important. An endocrinologist should be on the team for those with diabetes or thyroid disorders. If there is evidence of osteoporosis, an orthopedist (bone specialist) might be important. And almost all women should see a cardiologist at least once after menopause.

The tricky part, as most of us know, is finding professionals we feel comfortable with and establishing an honest working rapport. For those of us who grew up believing doctors were gods, this is no easy task.

Interviewing doctors makes most of us very uncomfortable. Yet, most doctors, if they were going to choose a doctor for themselves, wouldn't hesitate to interview a colleague. It's something like buying a car. You don't buy one without a test drive. The same is true when you select a physician.

The first step is to get recommendations from people you trust. If you are moving to a new town, ask your current doctor about doctors in the new location. Local libraries can be helpful, and many hospitals have referral services.

Once you've identified doctors you want to meet, make appointments and go in prepared to ask the questions most important to you. (Most doctors will not charge for this initial visit.)

Deciding what is important to you in a doctor-patient relationship may not be as easy as you think. Most of us wait until we are really sick before we seek medical attention. As we get older, however, we need to reshape our thinking and use the preventive approach. That means seeing a doctor BEFORE you get sick and taking steps to stop illness before it starts.

Many books and articles recommend that you go into the interview with a list. Be aware that lists do carry a bit of a risk. Many doctors have a very negative bias against the list-bearing patient. While doctors aren't necessarily taught that women wielding lists are neurotic, that idea has been perpetuated among many physicians.

During the menopausal years, many women are more comfortable with lists that help them stay right on track. And doctors need to be made aware of this. Our recommendation is to take an outline of how you want the interview to go. Refer to it discreetly, but let the doctor know that you are a major player on your health-care team and you want to have some role in making good use of your time with the doctor.

At the first meeting, you probably don't want to discuss all your symptoms. Instead you may want to find out how the doctor approaches various problems. Is he or she willing to talk about alternative therapies? What hospital is the doctor affiliated with? Is he or she accessible at off hours in the event of an emergency?

Beyond this, you'll want to learn something of the doctor's style of communication. Some women are more comfortable with the brisk, professional approach, while others want someone who is friendly and compassionate. You need someone with whom you can talk freely about your health care concerns. Developing a good rapport at this first meeting may pave the way for a healthy partnership.

As the primary caretakers of our bodies, it's important for each of us to learn as much as we can about health. Your doctor will never be the expert you are. You need to be in touch with your feelings, both physical and emotional, and you need to respond when you sense something is not quite right. Then you need to communicate your perceptions in a very clear and concise way.

Doctors can't deal with vague symptoms any better than you can. If you go to see the doctor saying, "I don't know, I just don't feel right," you will probably be sent home and told to take aspirin. If, on the other hand, you can identify some specific symptoms, you'll give the doctor something to go on that can lead to a correct diagnosis and treatment. For example, if you can say to the doctor, "I am getting headaches frequently. I've tracked them and I believe they occur at the same times as when I used to ovulate," you are providing good clues as to the source of the headaches.

To establish a good relationship with your doctor, try to be as prepared as possible before your appointment. Don't withhold information that may be important because you think it's embarrassing. Doctors don't embarrass easily. Your health is their business.

Respond appropriately when the doctor asks questions. So many of us are conditioned to be polite, and we don't always respond honestly. When your doctor asks how you are, try not to automatically answer "fine." You're probably there to solve a health problem that's a mystery for the doctor until the right information comes to light. Don't hold out. State the facts.

Finally, when the doctor comes up with a diagnosis, respect it. If you're given advice, follow it. But be sure to trust your own intuition as well. If you are convinced there is more to know, get another opinion.

WHAT TESTS DO YOU NEED?

As part of your own personal health management program, there are a number of screening tests you may want to schedule periodically to rule out various diseases. This list was compiled for "average women." If you are managing a chronic illness, you probably already have specific guidelines to follow. Ask your doctor about which tests are important for you. Together you can customize the list for your unique situation.

At a minimum, the following screenings should be considered:

1. Blood pressure check.—Blood pressure should be measured regularly throughout your life. High blood pressure is easily controlled once it has been detected, but if it is left untreated, it increases risks for coronary artery disease, stroke, and eye and kidney problems.

2. Breast exam.—You should be doing a breast self-exam monthly, but an annual exam by a trained health professional is recommended for all women age 40 and over.

3. Mammography.—All women age 50 and over should have an annual mammogram. If you're under 50, discuss your family history and other risk factors with your doctor and decide together how often this screening should be done.

4. Cholesterol readings.—A baseline test for total cholesterol and high- and low-density lipoproteins (HDL and LDL) should be done around age 50. If the results show you're within the normal limits, you won't need to be retested for 5 years or so. If either result is high, discuss your particular risks with your doctor and together set a reasonable testing schedule.

5. Electrocardiography (ECG)—This test records the electrical impulses of your heart and is usually recommended annually for women over age 65. You may want to consider a baseline screening at age 50 so you have a standard in your medical file for comparing future ECGs.

6. Fecal occult blood test.—This test requires you to follow a special diet and to collect stool samples. The samples are analyzed for blood from premalignant growths or colon or rectal cancers. The test is recommended annually for all people over age 50.

7. Pap smear.—After three consecutive annual tests showing normal results, this test is recommended at least every 3 years for sexually active women up to age 65. The Pap test is our best defense against cervical cancer.

8. Sigmoidoscopy.—In this procedure, a flexible tube is inserted into the rectum and colon to check for abnormalities. This test is recommended every 3 to 5 years beginning at age 50.

9. Skin examination.—During your annual physical, have the doctor look you over for skin cancer. The incidence of skin cancer is on the rise, and suspicious moles and marks on your skin should be evaluated for your protection.

In addition to these tests, periodic transvaginal sonography and endometrial sampling should be considered for post-menopausal women who are at high risk for uterine or endometrial or ovarian cancers.

To help your doctor evaluate your risk for cancer, osteoporosis, and heart disease, we've included some risk assessment forms in this chapter. These forms can help you determine if you are at low, moderate, or high risk for these disorders. We invite your comments, questions, and suggestions, and encourage you to discuss this information with your doctor.

CANCER

The annual evaluation of risk for cancer should include an assessment of high-risk habits, including smoking, exposure to second-hand smoke, excessive exposure to the sun, poor nutrition, use of drugs, use of estrogen, sexual practices, and history of sexually transmitted diseases. In addition, be sure your doctor knows about any family history of cancer.

Cancer is not just one disease. In fact, experts suspect cancer takes at least 100 different forms. It's possible to be at risk for one kind of cancer and not at all at risk for another. We've included some information on the various kinds of cancers along with a risk assessment profile for each. Score yourself to see where you stand. Then try to reduce your risk by practicing the behaviors or undergoing the treatments listed in the assessment. Talk to your doctor about these factors.

Breast cancer

The best defense against breast cancer is a program of monthly breast self-exams combined with regular clinical exams and mammography. Unfortunately, the incidence of breast cancer seems to be rising. Ten years ago, one in 10 women got breast cancer; today the figure is one in eight women. There is speculation that this rise is related to improvements in early detection, but the National Cancer Institute (NCI) is taking steps to find out exactly what's going on.

The NCI researchers theorize that the rise in breast cancer could be linked with a number of environmental changes, including compounds in drinking water, vehicle exhaust, chemicals formed in high-temperature cooking, and exposure to low-frequency electromagnetic fields. Pesticides containing DDT or PBBs (polybrominated biphenyls) and materials using PCBs (polychlorinated biphenyls) are among the prime suspects. All of these are known to increase the risk of cancer.

The NCI has undertaken five major studies in regions known for high exposure to environmental toxins. These studies will compare levels of carcinogens in blood and breast tissue from women who have developed breast cancer and those who haven't. While the real answers are years away, the NCI has at least begun to track the culprits in breast cancer.

You may find it interesting that these studies will focus on carcinogens and do not seem to implicate the use of estrogensand progesterone in breast cancer. That's because a major study involving all the previous studies done on the relationship between breast cancer and hormone replacement therapy showed that in the overwhelming majority of cases, the risk of breast cancer did not increase at all. A few studies showed a slightly increased risk for specific groups of women. The best available information, therefore, suggests that combined estrogen-progesterone therapy does not increase the risk of breast cancer.

The other pertinent risk factors are listed in the risk assessment profile that follows.

Duvivier Risk Assessment Profile for Breast Cancer

Circle the score if the statement is true for you.   *Score*

1. Under age 40	1
2. Age 40 to 55	2
3. Age over 55	3
4. Racial type: White	1
5. Racial type: Black	2
6. Early menarche (age under 10)	2
7. Late menopause (after age 55)	2
8. First pregnancy after age 35	2
9. Family history of breast cancer	2
10. Radiation exposure during prepubertal year	3
11. History of polycycstic ovary disease, pregnancy deficiency, or luteal phase defect	2
12. Obesity	2
13. Hypothyroidism	1
14. High dietary fat or hypercholesterolemia (high blood cholesterol)	2
15. Alcohol consumption over 5 oz./day hard liquor or 6 beer cans or more	1
16. Difficult breast self exam due to breast size, fibrocystic change, previous biopsies, previous surgery	2

17. Cancer in one breast   4

18. Never pregnant   2

19. Vitamin D or calcium deficiency   1

20. History of colon cancer   1

21. High socioeconomic status in developed country   1

Treatments and risk reduction (subtract numbers given)

1. Breast self-exam monthly   –3

2. Mammography periodically   –5

3. Breast exams by M.D. or R.N.   –3

4. Low dietary fat   –1

5. Low blood cholesterol   –1

6. High fiber/high calcium diet   –1

Add the circled numbers and subtract your risk reduction numbers.

Total score   _____

A score of less than 5 indicates a low risk.

From 6 to 10, risk increases to a moderate expectation.

A score of 11 or more is a clue to a high risk for breast cancer.

Endometrial or uterine cancer

An increased risk of endometrial or uterine cancer has been linked to the use of unopposed estrogen. This risk often discourages many women from using hormone replacement therapy. The facts show, however, that estrogen does not cause the cancer. It does, however, promote the growth of already cancerous cells. So women who take estrogen and then get endometrial cancer may have been predisposed to this cancer.

The important news is this: Combined hormone therapy, that is, estrogen combined with progesterone, does not increase the risk of endometrial cancer. In fact, it actually may reduce the risk.

And another important fact: Early endometrial cancers are rarely fatal. The cure rate today for a Stage I endometrial cancer is almost 100 percent. The fear of this cancer should no longer be a reason for not using hormone therapy if you need it.

You can evaluate your personal risk by using the profile below.

Duvivier Risk Assessment Profile for Endometrial (Uterine) Cancer

Circle the score if the statement is true for you.	*Score*
1. Age over 50	3
2. Menopause after age 55, menarche before 12	1
3. Never pregnant	2
4. Obesity (120% of ideal body weight), diabetes, hypertension	2
5. History of ovarian tumors or polycystic ovary disease, infertility	2

6. Liver disease   1

7. Thyroid disease   1

8. Breast cancer   2

9. Gastrointestinal cancer   1

10. History of endometrial hyperplasia   3

11. Estrogen treatment (unopposed)   5

Treatments and risk reduction (subtract numbers given)

1. History of use of combination oral
   birth control pills   −3

2. Progesterone/estrogen use   −3

3. Normal transvaginal sonograms
   and transvaginal color Doppler
   sonograms, or endometrial biopsy   −1

   *Add the circled numbers and subtract
   your risk reduction numbers.*

   Total score   _____

A score of 5 or less indicates a low risk.

Scores of 6 to 10 carry a moderate risk.

Scores of 11 points or more indicate high risk.

Ovarian cancer

Ovarian cancer is greatly feared among women today, particularly since by the time this cancer causes symptoms it is usually quite advanced. If you believe you are at risk, use the assessment form below and then discuss your fears with your doctor.

Duvivier Risk Assessment Profile for Ovarian Cancer

Circle the score if the statement is true for you.	*Score*
1. Age over 50	3
2. Family history of ovarian cancer	2
3. Turner syndrome with OX/OX mosaicism	2
4. Peutz-Jeghers syndrome	1
5. Multiple nevoid basal cell cancer syndrome (ovarian fibroma)	1
6. History of breast cancer	5
7. History of colon cancer	2
8. History of endometrial (uterine) cancer	2
9. High dietary animal fat (increased estrogen from gut bacteria)	1
10. Never pregnant	2
11. Talc use	1
12. Subclinical mumps oophoritis	1
13. Elevated gonadotropin-releasing hormone or FSH/LH	2

Treatments and risk reduction (subtract numbers given)

1. Oral birth control pills   –3

2. Transvaginal sonogram screening   –2

3. Normal CA-125, AFP, CEA levels   –1

> *Add the circled numbers and subtract your risk reduction numbers.*

Total score   _____

A score of 5 or less indicates a low risk.

From 5 to 10, risks are moderate.

Scores of 11 or above are associated with a high risk.

Cervical cancer

Cervical cancer is one of the most preventable of all the cancers. An annual Pap test is your best defense. Sadly, once women reach age 65, they seem to neglect this test, despite the fact that 40 percent of all deaths from cervical cancer are in older women.

Hormone replacement therapy does not increase the risk for cervical cancer. Also, women who have been diagnosed with cervical cancer are not at higher risk if they use hormone replacement. Use the following assessment form, then discuss the results with your doctor. And don't stop having those annual Pap tests.

Duvivier Risk Assessment Profile for Cervical Cancer

Circle the score if the statement is true for you.	*Score*
1. First intercourse before age 18	3
2. More than one sexual partner	3
3. One's partner has had several other partners	2
4. History of human papilloma virus, condyloma	3
5. Exposure to diethylstilbestrol (DES)	1
6. Use of oral birth control pills	1
7. Family history of cervical cancer	1
8. Cigarette smoking (one pack per day)	1
9. Passive smoking or exposure to tobacco smoke	1
10. Sex partner is a smoker	1
11. History of abnormal Pap smears	2
12. History of sexually transmitted diseases (gonorrhea, syphilis, trichomonas, herpes simplex virus, chlamydia, human immunodeficiency virus [HIV], or hepatitis)	2

Treatments and risk reduction (subtract numbers given)

1. Negative Pap smears for past 3 years	−3
2. Condom use	−3
3. Avoidance of tobacco	−1

4. Mutually monogamous sexual relationship   −2

5. Use of supplement of vitamins A and C   −1

Add the circled numbers and subtract your risk reduction numbers.

Total score   _____

A score of 5 or less indicates a low risk.

Scores of 6 to 10 carry a moderate risk.

Scores of 10 points or above indicate high risk.

OSTEOPOROSIS

Your bones may begin to change rapidly after menopause. Estrogen is a vital component in keeping bones strong and healthy. Most women reach their peak bone mass at about age 30, then begin to lose small amounts of bone as they age, beginning in their late 30s. After menopause, the process speeds up.

The most serious consequence of osteoporosis is the increased risk of bone fractures. In some women, bones break after minor injury or even during normal daily activity. There may be no symptoms of osteoporosis before a fracture occurs.

In the United States, nearly 700,000 people suffer hip fractures annually. By age 65, almost 25 percent of all white women have one or more fractures of the spine or hips. In most of these cases, the underlying cause of the fracture is osteoporosis.

Are you at risk?

To learn your personal risk of osteoporosis, we've included the following risk assessment profile. Use this form to evaluate where you stand, then discuss your risks with your doctor.

Duvivier Risk Assessment Profile for Osteoporosis

Circle the score if the statement is true for you.   *Score*

1 Female   2

2. Over age 60   1

3. Over age 70   2

4. Born prematurely (before 36 weeks
      or weighing less than 5 1/2 lbs.)   1

5. Oriental (Japan/China) or
      Caucasian from Northern Europe   2

6. Not breast fed as a baby   1

7. Already had natural menopause   2

8. Family history of osteoporosis   2

9. History of premature menopause
      (before age 40)

         —Medically induced   2

         —Surgically induced   4

         —Spontaneous or idiopathic (no reason)   1

10. a. Long-term treatment with steroids
         or anticonvulsants   4

       b. Long-term treatment with
          anticoagulants or thyroxin   1

       c. Long term treatment with tetracyclines   1

11. History of a easy fracture   6

12. Never had children or took no calcium
    supplements during pregnancy   1

13. History of hyperprolactinemia
    or prolonged lactation (breast
    feeding more than one year)   2

14. Multiple full-term pregnancies
    (more than 3) without calcium
    supplementation   2

15. Loose teeth, severe periodontal disease   2

16. Petite, slender, small stature   1

17. Scoliosis   1

18. Very high-fiber diet   1

19. Low dietary calcium (under 700 mg./day)   1

20. Low calcium retention (malabsorption,
    hypercalciuria)   2

21. High-protein diet (over 8 oz. red meat,
    poultry, fish, or eggs daily)   1

22. High caffeine intake (more than 2 cups
    of coffee daily)   1

23. High intake of alcoholic beverages
    (more than 5 oz./day)   2

24. Tobacco smoking or exposure to smoke   1

25. Low vitamin D intake or little sunshine
    exposure (less than 15 minutes/day)   1

26. Sedentary lifestyle or lack of daily
    aerobic or weight-bearing exercise   2

27. History of endometriosis or
    elevated interleukin 1   1

28. Low bone density with loss of height   5

29. History of hyperthyroidism   2

30. History of hyperparathyroidism   3

31. History of uremia   3

32. History of liver disease   3

33. History of lactose deficiency   2

Treatments and risk reduction (subtract numbers given)

1. Estrogen/progesterone use: orally,
   vaginally, transdermally, IM progesterone   −5

2. Calcium supplementation, good diet   −2

3. Vitamin D/sunshine   −1

4. Regular exercise   −3

5. Fluoride treatments   −1

6. Anabolic agents (Winstrol, Stanazolol)   −3

7. Calcitonin (Calcimar, USP, IM)
   with calcium and vitamin D   −3

8. Active diphosphonate, followed by a
   free period and then repeated   −3

9. Calcitrol therapy   −2

*Add the circled numbers and subtract
your risk reduction numbers.*

Total score _____

A score of 7 or less indicates a low risk.

From 8 to 10, risks are moderate.

At 11 or above, the risk for osteoporosis is high.

What to do about osteoporosis

Of course, hormone replacement therapy is recommended for the treatment of osteoporosis, as are exercise, supplemental calcium, and a high-calcium diet. A recent (1994) study poses a new and interesting theory about why osteoporosis is so prevalent in our later years. The study points out that when we are young, our blood is usually alkaline. As we age, our diet and metabolism change and blood becomes more acidic. The body looks for something to neutralize the acid in blood, and calcium can do that.

To test their theory, the researchers gave potassium bicarbonate to postmenopausal women on controlled diets. They learned that the oral administration of potassium bicarbonate at a dose sufficient to neutralize acid in the blood improved calcium and phosphorus balance, reduced bone resorption, and increased the rate of bone formation in these women. These are all good results.

The key in the study seemed to be the potassium bicarbonate. Yet other studies had tried a similar test in men using sodium bicarbonate and found no appreciable positive result. Watch for more news about this.

Another hopeful treatment, tested at the University of Texas Southwestern Medical Center, appears to actually rebuild bone. A low-dose (25 mg.), time-release form of sodium fluoride is taken with 400 mg. of calcium twice daily. While hormone replacement therapy slows the process of bone degeneration, it does not rebuild bone. This new treatment offers hope that the process can be reversed. Researchers hope to gain Food and Drug Administration approval soon.

HEART DISEASE, STROKE, AND OTHER CARDIOVASCULAR DISEASES

About 10 million American women suffer from myocardial vascular disease. Ten percent of women ages 45 to 64 have some form of it, and each year about 250,000 women die from it. Yet many women are completely unaware of the risk.

Until just a few years ago, heart disease was considered a man's disease. Women were virtually ignored in terms of research. Sadly, many physicians still aren't aware that women deserve and need as much, if not more, diagnostic testing, treatment, and follow-up for cardiovascular disorders as men. A woman who has a heart attack is almost twice as likely to die from it as a man.

What are the risk factors?

The same things that predispose men to heart disease apply to women: smoking, high blood pressure, obesity, and elevated serum cholesterol levels. Estrogen, however, appears to reduce risk, primarily by suppressing levels of low-density lipoprotein (LDL), which tends to accumulate in arterial plaque, and by raising levels of high-density lipoprotein (HDL), which clears cholesterol from the system. When estrogen levels fall during menopause, LDL creeps upward, HDL declines, and the risk of developing cardiovascular disease increases.

There are several good scientific studies that strongly suggest that hormone replacement protects the heart. But because there have been no large randomized clinical trials addressing the question of whether postmenopausal hormone treatment reduces the risk of cardiovascular disease in all women, some uncertainty remains about this issue.

Because of this, and because each year half a million American women die of cardiovascular disease, the American Fertility Society and the American Heart Association offered a "consensus opinion" in 1994, stating that hormone replacement therapy plays an important role in preventing heart disease in women.

In addition, the following risk factors were identified:

—Smoking

—Hypertension (high blood pressure)

—Impaired glucose tolerance and diabetes

—Dyslipidemia (high cholesterol, low HDL, high LDL, high triglycerides)

—Hyperandrogenism

—Old age

—Obesity

—Waist-to-hip ratio greater than 0.85

—Family history of cardiovascular disease

—History of cardiovascular events (stroke, transient ischemic attacks)

—History of chest pain

—Low socioeconomic status

—Hypercoagulopathy (blood that clots very easily)

—Chronic corticosteroid use

—Sedentary lifestyle

—Premenopausal bilateral oophorectomy
(removal of both ovaries)

—Premature ovarian failure

At the time of the conference, it was agreed that there just was not enough information to decide whether hormone replacement was too risky for some women, such as those with breast cancer.

What was agreed was that estrogens offer cardiovascular benefits. So far, however, we really don't know whether estrogen-progesterone treatment is as effective as unopposed estrogen in reducing the risk of heart disease in women; for the time being, we know that the addition of progesterone may reduce but does not eliminate the beneficial effects of estrogens.

Chest pain or angina seems to be a less reliable signal of heart disease in women than in men. In one study, half the women with chest pain had clear coronary arteries, while only 17 percent of the men did.

In another study, fewer women than men went on to have heart attacks. The chest pains and palpitations that some women experience as part of menopause seem unrelated to coronary heart disease. Yet it is always important to rule out heart disease. *Never ignore chest pains or palpitations!*

Noninvasive diagnostic procedures, such as exercise stress tests, and resting electrocardiography, may not be reliable for all women because criteria for these tests are based on statistical averages for men. The most definitive test, coronary angiography, is equally effective in identifying arterial obstructions in both sexes. Unfortunately, women are much less likely to be referred for coronary angiography than are men.

Most drugs to relieve angina or to dissolve blood clots in coronary arteries seem to be equally effective in men and women, according to recent data. However, clot-dissolving drugs are more likely to cause complications from bleeding in women. So far, we still don't know how hormone therapy affects the action of cardiovascular drugs or whether women, who have smaller hearts and body masses, need smaller doses.

We do know that women with coronary heart disease are less likely than men to undergo coronary-artery bypass surgery and balloon angioplasty, two procedures that improve blood flow to the heart. For unknown reasons, women seem less likely to benefit from angioplasty and more likely to have complications or to die from bypass surgery. We need to press for more research to discover what factors, such as age, anatomy, or coexisting conditions, are responsible for the poor outcomes for women.

At the conference cited above, the following questions were posed as research questions of the highest priority:

1. What are the risks and benefits of using combined estrogen-progesterone treatment? Of sequential regimens compared with continuous administration?

2. What are the effects of different routes of administration?

3. What is the impact of postmenopausal hormone therapy on particular subgroups of women, especially diverse socioeconomic groups, different ethnic and racial groups, and women with diabetes?

4. What are the important psychosocial factors that can affect cardiovascular disease? What is the role of modification of these factors?

5. How can we gain greater understanding of the biology of blood vessels and the pharmacologic effects of estrogens and progesterones?

6. Which progesterones and what doses are least likely to reverse the beneficial effects of estrogen while still protecting the endometrium?

7. How do dietary factors affect cardiovascular disease risk?

8. What are the effects of various hormonal regimens on breast cancer risk?

9. What is the impact of long duration of hormonal use? How long do effects persist after discontinuation?

10. Are there benefits to starting hormone therapy at different ages after menopause?

11. Is hormone replacement therapy neuroprotective?

It might take some time to gather answers, so watch for more information, and check with your physician for regular updates.

ALZHEIMER'S DISEASE

Research now also suggests that estrogen may be vitally important to the health of the human brain and may have a role in the prevention of Alzheimer's disease. The research, originally undertaken at the University of Southern California, indicates that women who take hormone replacement therapy are 40 percent less likely to develop Alzheimer's disease than women who are not on hormones.

It appears that estrogen assures the production of critical enzymes in the brain and helps maintain the densest possible mesh of fibers connecting one nerve cell to the next.

When estrogen levels drop at menopause, these brain connections may weaken, possibly making brain cells more likely to degenerate and die. This is significant in that Alzheimer's disease is a disorder apparently caused by the death of brain cells.

Women are known to suffer from this disease more often than men, yet men do not have life-long stores of estrogen. What's the difference? In aging men, a steady supply of testosterone may act as their safeguard against Alzheimer's. New research has shown that much of a man's circulating testosterone is converted to estrogen in the brain. Because men's testosterone levels do not dip sharply at any point and often stay reasonably high when men are well into their 80s, men could be getting the protective influence of estrogen in the brain for years.

Neurobiologists at Columbia University College of Physicians and Surgeons currently working on this research are convinced that estrogen participates in neural development and performance throughout life, helping to establish brain architecture in the fetus and then maintaining that intricate structure throughout adulthood.

While this research doesn't mean that all women over age 50 should immediately start taking hormones, it does introduce another area in which we need more information. When the pros and cons of taking hormone therapy are being evaluated, neurobiological health should go down on the plus side.

NEW EVIDENCE ABOUT VISION

In early 1994, a University of Wisconsin ophthalmologist, Barbara Klein, did a survey to find out if there was a link between estrogen replacement therapy and eye disease. She learned that women who took estrogen for at least five years following menopause reduced their risk of a common form of cataract by 10 percent. Those who took the hormone for 20 years reduced their risk of this cataract by 35 percent.

Granted, this is one study, and much more information is needed. Nonetheless, vision might be another entry on the plus side for hormone replacement therapy.

HOW ABOUT SEX?

Many women report that once the fear of pregnancy is over, they feel a new freedom in sexual relationships. Most older people want and are able to lead active, satisfying sex lives, according to a study begun at Duke University way back in 1954. Women do not ordinarily lose their physical capacity for orgasm with age. There is, however, a gradual slowing of response that is considered normal.

Women generally experience little loss of sexual capacity because of age alone. The changes that do occur, which affect the shape, flexibility, and lubrication of the vaginal area, can usually be traced directly to lower levels of estrogen once you have passed menopause.

Dealing with the changes

In terms of sex, as your estrogen levels decline, your clitoris may become slightly smaller and the lips of the vagina thinner and flatter. The covering of the clitoris may also pull back, leaving the area more exposed and increasingly more sensitive to touch. Vaginal tissues become drier and as a consequence, love-making may become less pleasant than it once was.

One of the most uncomfortable of all the results of menopause is vaginal dryness. It can be irritating, uncomfortable, or downright painful for many women, yet they may be uncomfortable talking about it with their doctors.

There are some things you can do on your own to relieve dryness and itching in this sensitive area. Over-the-counter products such as K-Y Jelly® or Astroglide®, help many women. These water-based lubricants offer advantages over oil-based products because they are less likely to encourage bacterial growth that might lead to infection. Replens® is another over-the-counter product advertised as effective in restoring vaginal moisture, but only when it is used regularly.

Estrogen creams are also very helpful in resolving vaginal dryness, but you do need a doctor's prescription to get them. Used about three times a week, estrogen cream goes directly to the source of the discomfort and, over time, can begin to revive these tissues and help them retain moisture.

You'll want to be careful not to use estrogen cream immediately before love making, however, since it is a powerful hormone and it may be absorbed into your partner's body instead of your own. Talk to the doctor about your symptoms, and get advice on how to use the cream.

Some things you may want to avoid include douches, perfumed bath soaps and oils, long hot baths in perfumed suds, scented toilet paper, and lotions that will further dry you out.

Also, be careful with antihistamine use. Antihistamines dry many tissues in the body in addition to those you want dried. Other medications may also result in vaginal dryness, and you need to know exactly what you are taking and how it can affect your body.

WHAT ARE YOU DOING THE REST OF YOUR LIFE?

At this time, more than 30 percent of the postmenopausal women in the U.S. are on hormone replacement therapy. But many will discontinue hormones for one reason or another. Because the main goal of hormone replacement therapy is not just getting through menopause but ensuring a healthy future, please do your best to give the treatment a fair trial. If you decide to stop taking hormones or any other medication, always talk it over with your doctor.

Orthopedic and cardiovascular benefits accrue after at least five years, but how long should hormone therapy continue? That is still an open question. The most recent evidence suggests that the protection against osteoporosis seems to disappear once the therapy is withdrawn.

Using hormone therapy to maintain healthy bones seems to work at any age after menopause. Evidence suggests it's never too late to start. If you're already affected by osteoporosis, ask your doctor about starting hormone replacement therapy to hold the disease at bay. You will not reverse osteoporosis, but you can slow it down.

Until we have more scientific information, it seems reasonable to say that the reasons you started taking hormones in the first place should help you decide how long to stay on the treatment. If your main concern is a transient dryness of the vagina or the discomfort caused by hot flashes and night sweats, you may want to stop treatment when those problems have been alleviated.

On the other hand, if you are at high risk for cardiovascular disease or osteoporosis, hormone therapy may have to be continued indefinitely, until we know better, until we discover something superior, or " 'til death do us part."

The issues discussed in this chapter are serious concerns for your healthy future. Talk to your primary health care team, get all the information available, assess your personal risks in each instance, and then make the decision that promises you the most healthful future.

$\mathcal{F}$OOD
FOR THOUGHT

"$\mathcal{M}$y recurring fantasy isn't about Paul Newman or Robert Redford," Ginny confessed as we puffed through our morning walk at the mall. "It's about food. I dream about a machine that eats fat. It looks like one of those metal detectors at the airport. But when you walk through, all excess fat cells are instantly vaporized. It keeps me at an ideal weight while preserving everything my body needs to stay healthy. Oh, and it infuses self-esteem, confidence, poise, and good judgment."

Would that it could be! But until such a machine comes along, how can we handle weird food cravings, carbohydrate binges, fat flings, protein pig-outs, and bread bashes?

This whole food thing gets more confusing with each passing day. In fact, just a few months ago, we thought we had some answers to maintaining optimum health: cut back on fats, increase carbohydrates, and add fiber. Then, just days ago, somebody announced carbohydrates are dangerous because they speed up insulin production. This leads to a state of insulin resistance, which makes your body more likely to convert dietary calories into body fat. On top of that, we're told 25 percent of Americans may be insulin resistant, including the majority of overweight people.

At midlife, few women (none that we know) believe their weight is what it should be. In our minds, every single one of us is overweight, and dieting is a national pastime. In our heads we know dieting doesn't work, and good nutrition is what matters. But many of us still hang on to bad eating habits.

FOOD AND AGING

When it comes to life expectancy, it's no surprise that females fare better than males. Women tend to live five to nine years longer than men, but they don't necessarily live healthier. Just check out your local nursing home. About 80 percent of its residents will be women.

As we've said before, living longer isn't what it's all about. The trick is living better. And the longer we choose to live with healthful habits, the better off we should be. The time to start is now, while you're young enough to reverse some of the changes that might be looming. Most experts agree that good food choices make a profound difference in the quality of life as well as the length of life.

Aging is caused by a loss of functioning cells, especially the muscle and nerve cells, which have a limited capacity to regenerate. A number of theories have been developed to explain how cell loss occurs, including the waste-products theory, the immune theory, the cross-linkage theory, and the free-radical theory. This last one has attracted a lot of attention in recent years.

Evidence is growing to support the idea that highly reactive molecules called free radicals are implicated in both aging and disease. These substances are unavoidable. They are formed by radiation and herbicides. In addition, they exist in polluted air, ozone, tobacco smoke, and some types of fats. They are also generated through biological processes, including normal oxygen metabolism.

Oxygen is the body's most important "nutrient." We can live weeks without carbohydrates or protein and days without water. But without oxygen, we die in a matter of minutes. Paradoxically, oxygen is also the main source of free radicals. While the analogy is crude, we could think of oxygen as the "rust" factor when it comes to aging. The more technical term for rusting of cells is "oxidative cell damage."

Free radicals attack cells and block their ability to produce energy. They also damage the cells' genetic code. This whole process leads to a loss in the number of normal cells and deterioration of the tissues. Eventually the damaged cells die. Free radicals also attack fat cells, especially low-density lipoprotein (LDL). The damaged LDL remains in the blood longer than normal, increasing the risk for damage to blood vessels and vital organs.

Fortunately, the body also has a defense mechanism for warding off the effects of free radicals. This "antioxidant" system uses enzymes, vitamins, and minerals. If you have tuned in to the great vitamin debate lately, you're no doubt aware of the interest in antioxidant foods. These foods are rich in vitamins A (beta carotene), C, and E; the mineral selenium; and bioflavonoids, which are pigments most often found in the skins of fruits and vegetables.

The new thinking encourages everyone—men, women, boys, and girls—to concentrate on eating more fruits and vegetables (many of which contain antioxidants) and cut back on fats.

WHERE DO WE GET ANTIOXIDANTS?

When it comes to protecting our bodies from free-radicals, vitamin E is an extremely valuable asset. It protects against environmental toxins found in polluted air and prevents free-radical damage to tissues. Almonds, avocado, broccoli, wheat germ and wheat germ oil, cottonseed oil, safflower oil, whole-grain cereals, and whole-wheat breads are good sources.

Vitamin C plays an important role in reducing the risk for a number of diseases. Good sources include asparagus, beet greens, broccoli, brussels sprouts, cabbage, cantaloupe, collard greens, grapefruit and grapefruit juice, green peas, green peppers, oranges and orange juice, red bell peppers, strawberries, and tomato juice.

Beta carotene, or vitamin A, is an extremely potent antioxidant. Some research shows that one molecule of beta carotene can destroy more than a thousand free radical molecules. Beta carotene also seems to help prevent formation of the free radicals in the first place. Foods rich in beta carotene include apples, apricots, asparagus, beet greens, brussels sprouts, cantaloupe, carrots and carrot juice, celery, collard greens, sweet potatoes, peaches, romaine lettuce, spinach, and winter squash.

Selenium strengthens the immune system and fends off free radical attacks. Studies have shown that diets low in selenium often lead to high numbers of free radicals in tissues. Selenium is found in chicken without the skin, lean meat, nonfat milk, organ meats, seafood, vegetables, whole-grain cereals, and whole-wheat bread.

MAKING CHANGES

The bottom line for most of us is this: We consume too much fat in our diets and don't eat enough nutrient-dense fruits and vegetables. It is mostly the fat in our diet that begets fat in our bodies. Fat promotes heart disease, some types of cancer, diabetes, and obesity.

In spite of all our dieting, Americans are becoming more obese, not less. C. Everett Koop, former surgeon general, places nutrition at the forefront in our defense against chronic illness. He points out that, as Americans, our greatest health concern is excessive intake of dietary fat and its relationship to the risk of chronic diseases.

So, while we do not advocate dieting, we advocate a low-fat food plan rich in vitamins and minerals that will sustain your good health for the rest of your life.

FIGURING OUT FATS

Fat is sneaky. It turns up in so many things that appear so innocent—even healthy. Frozen yogurt, for example, isn't necessarily fat free. And popcorn, a wonderful high-fiber treat, can be loaded with fat.

The new food labels provide excellent information for tracking fat. But sometimes they are confusing because they look at percentages of daily values for an average population, rather than for you as an individual. The following information may help you figure out your own needs.

As a general rule, dietitians recommend that no more than 30 percent of calories each day come from fat. One gram of fat contains 9 calories. So, let's say you eat 1,800 calories in a day. When you multiply 1,800 calories by 30 percent, you get 540 calories. That's the *maximum* number of fat calories you should eat daily.

To translate that into grams, divide 540 by 9 (the number of calories in a gram of fat), and you learn that your daily intake of fat should not exceed 60 grams.

Now, some nutritionists say 60 grams of dietary fat daily is on the high side. You want to ask your doctor, dietitian, or nutritionist to help you fine-tune the formula for your body. Many experts now recommend a 20 percent limit for fat calories, but be careful not to go too low. Your body does need some fat to function properly. Most of the current information says never to go below 17 percent of calories from fat, but here again, more research is needed to explain exactly what is best as we get older.

In addition to too much fat, most American diets are sadly lacking in fiber. Bran cereals, whole grains, rice and breads, and legumes (beans, lentils, split peas) are all good sources. And, of course, most fruits and vegetables contain fiber as well.

When you eat, try to fill up on plant foods first. Try to have at least five servings of fruits and vegetables every day. Concentrate on vegetables that are deeply colored—broccoli, peppers, green beans, tomatoes, sweet potatoes, and carrots. If you love desserts, try to use fruits more often and fats less frequently.

HINTS FOR HEALTHFUL EATING

Here are some more hints for hitting the five-a-day fruit and vegetable quota:

1. Start meals with thick vegetable soup made from leftover vegetables. Puree them in your food processor for a thick broth, or add them whole to clear broth.

2. Toss chopped vegetables like green peppers, radishes, carrots, or cucumbers into your tuna or egg salad sandwiches.

3. Stir-fry broccoli, pea pods, bean sprouts, sweet red peppers, and mushrooms. Use them in omelettes, rolled up in tortillas, or as a side dish. (Go easy on the oil when you stir-fry.)

4. Replace cream sauces with fruit or vegetable salsas for use with poultry, fish, or pork.

5. Top low-fat angel food cake with fresh or canned chopped fruits mixed with low-fat yogurt for a delicious low-calorie dessert.

6. Keep a bowl of fresh fruit on the table for snacking, and always have some cleaned carrots or celery in the refrigerator when you need to crunch between meals.

7. Use low-fat, calcium-rich dairy foods like low-fat yogurt, skim milk, cottage cheese, and their derivatives, such as frozen yogurt or ice milk, in place of the more calorie-dense versions.

GAINING WEIGHT

Most women gain weight during the perimenopausal years. The pendulum seems to shift monthly as to whether this is normal and perhaps even healthy or whether it is truly hazardous to health.

Some experts have recently said a pound a year weight gain is actually healthy as we get older. But as soon as that information was published, another study showed that the risk of heart disease goes up significantly when weight goes up, even if that weight gain is very small.

As we said earlier, thin women seem to have more symptoms of menopause than heavier women. And thin women are known to be at a higher risk for osteoporosis. If weight is a key focus of your life—and it is for most women—try not to be too hard on yourself during these years. Keep in mind that quick weight loss can be dangerous, and most weight loss gimmicks don't work. Slow and easy is best.

A chart recently developed by the National Institute of Aging, Gerontology Research Center, shows the expected weight ranges for healthy men and women at various ages. (Healthy means free of chronic diseases such as high blood pressure, arthritis, diabetes, or high cholesterol.) The lower figure in each range is for people with small frames and the higher is for those with large frames. These numbers are considerably more generous than the old insurance tables. While this information is still being debated by researchers, we've included it here to show you that normal weights are expected to change over the years.

EXPECTED WEIGHT RANGES FOR MEN AND WOMEN (IN POUNDS) BY AGE GROUP

HEIGHT	AGE 25	AGE 35	AGE 45	AGE 55	AGE 65
4'10"	84-111	92-119	99-127	107-135	115-142
4'11"	87-115	95-123	103-131	111-139	119-147
5'0"	90-119	98-127	106-135	114-143	123-152
5'1"	93-123	101-131	110-140	118-148	127-157
5'2"	96-127	105-136	113-144	122-153	131-163
5'3"	99-131	108-140	117-149	126-158	135-168
5'4"	102-135	112-145	121-154	130-163	140-173
5'5"	106-140	115-149	125-159	134-168	144-179
5'6"	109-144	119-154	129-164	138-174	148-184
5'7"	112-148	122-158	133-169	143-179	153-190
5'8"	116-153	126-163	137-174	147-184	158-196
5'9"	119-157	130-168	141-179	151-190	162-201
5'10"	122-162	134-173	145-184	156-195	167-207
5'11"	126-167	137-178	149-190	160-201	172-213
6'0"	129-171	141-183	153-195	165-207	177-219

Source: National Institute of Aging, Gerontology Research Center

LOSING WEIGHT

Don't you hate those smug people who tell you losing weight is easy? We just have to eat less and exercise more, they sniff.

Right! Easy for them to say. Some of them actually *forget* to eat every now and then. See how sympathetic we are when they starve to death!

We're here to tell you losing weight is not easy, especially for midlife women. Our bodies are very efficient at storing fat for times of famine. The only problem is we haven't had a famine for some years now. Most of us have never even been seriously hungry. So what do we have to do to lose those extra pounds?

Sorry to have to bear the bad news, but we're convinced the only thing that works in the long run is a combination of low-fat, nutrient-dense meals and exercise. That dreaded "E" word again.

Jo Gabrielson, a much-loved Weight Watchers leader in the Twin Cities, tells about her experience with exercise.

"I finally had to do something about my very serious weight problem," she tells other Weight Watchers. "I weighed twice what I should and knew my health was in jeopardy. So I suited up and put the leash on my six-pound dog. Together we headed out the door. I thought a six-block walk would be an easy start. Well, about three blocks out, I was sure I was going to die. The only thing that kept me moving was a vision of the police spray-painting the outline of my body on the street. It could be there for years, I thought. If I'm going to die, it has to be at home. And so I pushed myself to the limit and made the six blocks."

To her amazement, when Jo finished her walk, a neighbor called to ask if it was Jo she had seen out walking that morning.

"Awfully nice of her," Jo remarks, "since at that time we had very few 300-pound women with six-pound dogs in our neighborhood." The neighbor asked if she could walk with Jo the next day, and before long others also joined in. "That was one of the nicest things I ever did for myself," Jo adds.

When we were children, we didn't think about exercising. We just ran, skated, jumped rope, and had fun. We called it playing. But as we got older, we made exercise into something negative, even referring to it as "working out." If we could get back into that playful mode, more of us probably could truly enjoy exercise. So, if you see your neighbor out walking, ask if you can play, too.

MORE ABOUT CALCIUM

We haven't found any arguments about the belief that our need for calcium increases with age. Food is always the best source of calcium, but it can be difficult to get all your calcium from food every day. Try to incorporate more calcium-rich foods among your vegetable and protein choices, but ask your doctor about a supplement if you are concerned about getting enough calcium.

You should know that although spinach has a lot of calcium, it's not a great source because it also contains something called oxalates. These substances interfere with your body's ability to absorb calcium.

Calcium is absorbed better if you eat calcium-rich foods as part of a complete meal. Also, watch your caffeine intake. Caffeine causes the body to excrete calcium. A 1990 study showed that the risk of hip fracture was increased by 53 percent in people who drank two cups of coffee or four or more cups of tea daily.

SOURCES OF CALCIUM

FOOD	AMOUNT	CALORIES	CALCIUM
CHEESE			
SWISS	1 OZ.	105	272 MG.
PROVOLONE	1 OZ.	100	214 MG.
PARMESAN	1 TBSP.	25	69 MG.
COTTAGE CHEESE			
LOW-FAT	1 CUP	205	155 MG.
CREAMED (4%)	1 CUP	235	135 MG.
MILK			
SKIM	1 CUP	85	302 MG.
WHOLE	1 CUP	120	291 MG.
YOGURT			
PLAIN, LOW-FAT	8 OZ.	145	415 MG.
SEAFOOD			
SHRIMP	3 OZ.	100	98 MG.
VEGETABLES			
BROCCOLI, RAW	1 SPEAR	40	172 MG.
COLLARDS, COOKED	1 CUP	50	357 MG.
KALE, COOKED	1 CUP	35	179 MG.

DRINK YOUR WATER

Older bodies need more fluids to avoid dehydration and to dilute toxins and move them out of the body. Try to drink at least eight 8-ounce cups of noncaffeinated, noncarbonated beverages daily. Soups, fruits, and vegetables contain generous quantities of water, but try to get in the habit of drinking extra fluids as well.

WHAT ABOUT PHYTOCHEMICALS?

Phytochemicals, or chemicals produced by photosynthesis in plants (*phyto* is the Greek word for plant), are being rediscovered today, even though people have been eating them for thousands of years. Among the phytochemicals is a natural estrogen called, not surprisingly, phytoestrogen.

Women in China and Japan rarely complain of any of the host of symptoms associated with menopause. Hot flashes are virtually unknown in these populations. Because the Asian diet contains large amounts of soy products, researchers wondered if there could be a possible relationship. They learned soybeans, as well as soybean derivatives, such as tofu, contain— you guessed it—phytoestrogens.

Besides phytoestrogens, you might want to learn more about the phytochemicals listed below, that also benefit women.

Capsaicin, found in hot peppers, is reputed to protect DNA from carcinogens, much like the antioxidants.

Coumarins, found in citrus fruit and tomatoes, are believed to stimulate anticancer enzymes and prevent blood clotting.

Flavonoids, found in citrus fruit, tomatoes, berries, peppers, and carrots, are said to prevent cancer-promoting hormones from attaching themselves to normal cells and to inhibit enzymes responsible for cancer cell metastasis.

Genistein, found in beans, peas, and lentils, is reported to inhibit estrogen-promoted cancers.

Indoles, found in broccoli and members of the cabbage family, are said to protect against breast and prostate cancers.

Isothiocyanates, found in broccoli, cabbage, mustard, and horseradish, are reputed to stimulate anticancer enzymes and protect against breast cancer.

Lignins are found in flaxseed, barley, and wheat, and are believed to act as antioxidants, stimulating enzymes that detoxify cancer cells.

Lycopene, found in tomatoes and red grapefruit, is said to act as an antioxidant and to protect against cervical cancer.

S-allycysteine, found in garlic, onions, and chives, is believed to stimulate anticancer enzymes and block formation of nitrite in the stomach.

Triterpenoids, found in licorice root and citrus fruit, are reported to inhibit hormone-dependent steps in tumor formation.

Researchers have been intrigued by phytochemicals for years; they hope phytochemicals will provide a nontoxic approach to building up the immune system and supporting other body functions.

There is one big concern with using phytoestrogenic foods as a sole supplemental hormone source. While phytoestrogens in food can help with the symptoms, they do not seem to offer the same long-term protection against osteoporosis that hormone replacement therapy offers. Again, this is the time to check with your doctor about what is best for you.

CHAPTER VII

RECLAIMING YOUR PASSION

Mama Squirrel decided it was time for little Sally to get some education. So she sent her off to school. There Sally met Felicia Fish and Sarah Sparrow, and all soon became friends. The teacher, wise old Olivia Owl, noticed Sally excelled in running, Felicia was an excellent swimmer, and Sarah could fly to great heights. "Well," Olivia thought to herself, "I once again have my work cut out for me. My job is to find my students' weaknesses and improve performance in those areas. But why any fish needs to learn to fly is beyond me."

Life certainly involves challenging ourselves to do better in areas where we are weak. But too often we wind up doing things we don't enjoy or aren't very good at, simply because some subtle influence has convinced us that's the way to build "character."

Amid all the changes going on around menopause, many women are confronted with thoughts about what they have done with their lives. And with those thoughts come concerns about whether it's too late to do anything differently. Maybe you heard about the 101-year-old woman who stayed in a miserable marriage because she didn't want to divorce her husband until the kids were dead! Lots of women get themselves into similar predicaments, waiting to take care of themselves until they run out of excuses.

EVERYTHING'S COMING UP ROSES

While this book is mostly about menopause, the heart of the message is this: There is life, and lots of it, after menopause. Midlife need not be a crisis. Change is a good catalyst for moving us out of old molds and shooting us into new realms of exciting activity in the years ahead.

Midlife, even with its inherent madness, leads us into a new life arena, one filled with freedoms we never had an opportunity to enjoy before.

"I used to care a great deal what other people thought of me," our friend Peggy confided. "But today, I'm really free of all that. I care what I think of me, and I'm off to do what I choose to do. It doesn't matter what my kids think or what my colleagues think. It matters what I think."

Peggy went off to work as a volunteer on an archaeological dig in the jungles of Mexico—at age 63. Her children were afraid she would get hurt. Peg was afraid that if she didn't do what she wanted to do, she would always resent having missed making her life her own. So off she went.

Another friend joined the Peace Corps at age 58. She studied nursing and today is working in a field hospital somewhere in South America. Then there's Betty. She's 64. She took some painting lessons last year and found her passion. Now she's having a one-woman show at a local art center. She's planning on taking a trip next year to the South of France, just to paint.

"Okay," you're probably saying, "It's easy for those women. They don't have the challenges I have in my life." But it can't hurt to take a good look at those challenges. Do you really have full responsibility for them? Do you not have the right to take your life back?

Now is a good time to think about your own needs and make them a priority. Your mate will be fine. Your kids will be fine—and if they're not, you probably wouldn't have had any control over their lives anyway. Now it's your turn.

Maybe leisure time activity isn't your bag. There are lots of women who begin careers after menopause.

A very interesting study of working women, ages 55 to 74, found that they had lower cholesterol and blood sugar and better blood pressure and insulin levels than a matched group of women who did not work outside of their homes. The working women seemed to drink less, smoke less, weigh less, and exercise more.

Researchers speculate that working gave these women some kind of psychological bonus that led to good health. In addition, these women had more effective support structures, more friends with whom they shared their lives and their stresses.

So, perhaps it's time for you to think of launching a career. Or find your own personal passion and go for it! Even if the job market looks bleak, there's likely to be a spot for you.

Moments of Madness

•

"YOU CAN LEAD A FISH TO WATER, BUT YOU HAVE TO WALK REALLY FAST OR IT WILL DIE!"

—ROSE, ON THE GOLDEN GIRLS

One of the best ways to get into the job you want is to try volunteering for the association or group. Many of the women we know who wanted (or needed) to work got great jobs by volunteering first.

Look around you. There are places everywhere that need your special services. Do you think you don't have anything to offer? Think again. You've managed your life all these years, you've quite possibly kept a home, or paid the rent, or raised some kids, or survived a marriage or two, or successfully cemented a lasting relationship with one special person. All of this takes talent in today's world.

Give yourself credit for all the meals, all the loads of laundry, all the carpooling, all the PTA meetings, all the homework counseling, all the late-night fretting, all the concern and love you've delivered to all those important people in your life. You'll discover you're one special woman! And you have lots more to give.

PUT ON A HAPPY FACE

Now we come to really interesting stuff. If you're not happy, a unique way to help yourself cope is to *pretend* you are happy. A recent report in *Psychological Science* revealed that smiling stimulates certain muscles in the face, triggering increased activity in the brain that helps you actually feel happy. So smiling, even when you don't feel like it, can actually put you in a better mood. If you feel down, fake it. Pretend you feel up, and pretty soon chances are you will.

Other tips to make you feel better about yourself and your life: remember, it's never too late to start an exercise program. Our friend Mary took up cross-country skiing at age 65. She'd never even taken a long walk to our knowledge, and today she's devoted to her strenuous sport. Then there's Patty. She began lifting weights when she turned 58. Today she is more fit than she was in her 30s, and she feels great.

By the way, another benefit of exercise is related to breast cancer. In the years after menopause when the ovaries shut down, most of the body's estrogen comes from fat cells. That's also the time when breast cancer rates skyrocket. Using exercise to convert that body fat to lean muscle tissue becomes an excellent defense against this cancer that threatens so many women.

We also know that moderate exercise stimulates the immune system, and by keeping the immune system healthy, we can ward off other diseases. Finally, the benefits of weight-bearing exercise in maintaining healthy bones have been well documented.

So, you see, there are lots of reasons to get going, right away, on a good exercise program and a low-fat, high-fiber eating regimen. We don't mean to preach, but if you get nothing else out of this book, you'll know that there's a very important link between what you eat, what you do physically, and how long and how well you'll live after menopause.

SLEEPING WITH THE ENEMY

There is indeed an enemy that we all confront at midlife—STRESS! Stress is a normal part of everyone's life, and the midlife years tend to be pretty stressful. However, it's not the stress itself that's harmful; it's how we respond to the stress. When we drink too much, use drugs, or lash out at those who love us, we are probably responding inappropriately to stress. Finding more positive ways to "vent" stress seems in order at midlife.

Humor is one way of reducing or relieving stress. It promotes both psychological and physical well-being and provides a positive way of looking at our problems.

Hans Selye, an Austrian endocrinologist, spent years studying stress and its effects on the human body. After more than 50 years of research, he was able to say with certainty, "Nothing erases unpleasant thoughts more effectively than concentration on pleasant ones."

Humor can help us perceive the ridiculous, the absurd, and the incongruous. We can use humor to deal with our setbacks in a positive way, and to forestall those times when we feel sorry for ourselves. If we can laugh, others will be more likely to laugh with us and not pity us for our misfortune.

Several body systems are affected by laughter. The heart, lungs, and other muscles are stimulated, similar to what happens with aerobic exercise, and oxygen exchange is improved. Laughter also promotes the release of endorphins in the brain. Endorphins are "feel-good" chemicals that foster a sense of relaxation and well-being.

> *Moments of Madness*
>
> •
>
> "IF YOU LOVE SOME-ONE, SET THEM FREE.
>
> IF THEY COME BACK, THEY'RE PROBABLY BROKE."
>
> —RHONDA DICKISON

While researchers are still looking at what happens in our brains and bodies when we laugh, there's no question among today's medical practitioners: *Laughter complements medicine.* Of course, there are many types of humor. Some are more appropriate than others. Ethnic humor tends to be insulting. Black humor can be macabre. Sarcasm, our least favorite, isn't really funny at all. The best humor emerges all by itself. Something happens, and you find the humor in it. That's healthy humor.

The *Mayo Clinic Health Letter* gives the following suggestions for promoting humor in your life:

1. Be open to humor; give yourself permission to laugh or smile or to find a moment of pleasure, especially during difficult times.

2. Keep a daily humor journal with positive, unexpected joys that come into your life.

3. Nurture your sense of humor; focus on the positive.

4. Find your funny bone. Emphasize those things that help you to laugh. Downplay the rest.

5. Be gentle with yourself—try a smile first. Then give yourself a standing ovation (ovulation?) and get ready for a full-blown belly laugh.

6. Make a list of 20 items that bring you pleasure and amusement. Call it your fun-things-to-do list. Post it. Select something to do each day. Write a new list each month.

7. Look for humor in everyday happenings, and it will find you.

This concept of humor for good health is not new. In the Bible, Proverbs 17:22, it says, "A cheerful heart is good medicine, but a crushed spirit dries up the bones." In 1979, the relationship between humor and health became apparent through Norman Cousins' book called *Anatomy of an Illness.* Cousins was diagnosed with ankylosing spondylitis, a usually irreversible, arthritis-related disease that attacks the body's connective tissues.

Cousins augmented his medical therapy with massive doses of vitamin C, a positive attitude, and humor therapy. He reported, "Ten minutes of genuine belly laughter had an anesthetic effect and would give me at least two hours of pain-free sleep." Since then, the relationship between laughter and health has been the subject of many studies. A new specialty, gelotology, or humor physiology, has even sprung up.

We know that sitting around and laughing all day is impractical, but developing a dependable sense of humor can be mighty handy when dealing with your fears about the future. We have a club around here that requires each member to bring in a fresh joke every day. That guarantees us at least one good laugh a day. And that's good medicine.

So, what does all this mean? It means that you need to find fun and make a big place in your life for it. Have some fun every single day. Fun can be your personal management tool for handling stress. Try it, it works!

MORE TIPS FOR MANAGING YOUR NEW LIFE

You're ready to face the future. You've inventoried your life, and you've identified your passions, the things you can't imagine living without. You're ready to set the past aside. Here are some tips:

• *Don't relive the past.* Get rid of your baggage and don't assume the future will be anything like the past.

• *Accept yourself just the way you are.* You're probably not perfect, so don't expect yourself to be.

• *Break the guilt habit.* Eliminate the word "should" from your vocabulary and never reevaluate your actions negatively. Replace recrimination with observation. Tell yourself, "I handled that well." "I learned a lot from that experience."

• *Learn to say no.* And say it without guilt. You don't need to explain your answer or defend yourself. Just say no.

• *Give yourself the freedom to change your mind.* Reassessing a situation is a mark of flexibility, not instability.

• *Become your own permission-giver.* Allow yourself, with enthusiasm, to take a nap, go on a vacation, read a book, listen to music, watch television. Do it all without guilt. There's nothing more important than taking care of yourself right now.

• *Set realistic limits.* Underachieve, underschedule, and even underwhelm yourself. Don't worry, there's still plenty to do.

• *Become your own best friend.* Look out for yourself and protect yourself from stress, just like you protected your loved ones all your life. Take good care of you.

• *Create your own self-fulfilling prophecies by expecting the best!*

• *Figure out how to forgive others.* Harboring hostility has been proved to be damaging to the heart—yours, not the one belonging to the person who offended you. Think carefully about whether it's in your best interest to hold a grudge.

Moments of Madness

•

WHATEVER YOU'RE DOING, IT'S NOT AS IMPORTANT AS PLAYING WITH THE CAT.

T-SHIRT SLOGAN

• *Finally, laugh, laugh, laugh!* Produce those life-giving endorphins. They can give you good health and a happy time; they promote healing and reduce stress; they relax your muscles and restore your objectivity. And they foster hope and brighten the future for you and everyone around you.

CHAPTER VIII

PLANTING THE TREE OF KNOWLEDGE

As you think about your own midlife experience, you'll probably agree that the most difficult part is not knowing what to expect or when to expect it. Our mothers didn't discuss the subject. But today's women are not likely to hide in their bedrooms until they feel better. We all have places to go and things to do. One way to improve the situation is to share information with each other and especially with our own daughters. If knowledge truly is power, let's empower the next generation of women by telling them what we've learned.

An excellent way to start is by keeping a diary of your symptoms and feelings. Note when they started and how long they lasted. Jot down what you did about them and what worked or didn't work. If you don't want to keep a diary, make notes in the margins of this book, highlight things you can relate to, attach a sticky note, or put a check beside items that concern you. Then pass the book along to your daughter, or share it with your friends.

Keeping a journal can do more than just preserve the experience for your daughters and granddaughters. It can be a cathartic agent that is both healing and revealing. You'll find you know a lot more about your body than you ever realized. You may also learn you have pretty good coping skills and perhaps more control over your life than you realized.

MENOPAUSAL SYMPTOMS JOURNAL

Perhaps you'll want to use a more formal method of recording than just the margins of this book. Below is a suggested format for a typical symptoms journal. If you opt for this tool, you may want to use some sort of a scale of severity. Here is one example:

> 1 = not noticeable
>
> 2 = mild, needing no treatment
>
> 3 = moderately uncomfortable, requiring some attention
>
> 4 = severe and interfering with lifestyle, needing treatment

Start by recording your symptoms, and then note the following about each symptom:

> When did you first notice the symptom?
>
> What is its frequency?
>
> How has it affected your life?
>
> What are you doing about it?

Pick only those symptoms that apply to you, but remember, the perimenopause is a dynamic time of your life and these effects may change from time to time.

A list of common symptoms is on the next page.

Make notes about the following, or about any symptoms affecting you.

Hot flashes

Flushing

Increased perspiration

Palpitations

Insomnia

Mood swings

Relationship to periods:

Relationship to diet:

Heavy periods

Light or missed periods

Irritability

Depression

Vaginal itching/burning

Vaginal discharge

Vaginal dryness

Painful intercourse

Note any other symptoms you experience. Try to record just enough detail to show the relationship between symptoms and your cycles.

Note any other factors that affect symptoms.

Stress

Hormone treatments

Physical conditions or environment

Diet

Smoking

Alcohol consumption

Major life changes

Death of a loved one

Divorce

Job changes

Financial status changes

Many factors in your life affect your menstrual cycle. Emotions seem to be directly linked with hormonal activity, but as yet medical science doesn't agree on which is the cart and which the horse. Do you feel out of sorts because your hormones are changing, or are your hormone levels changing because you feel out of sorts?

Tracking the relationship of your feelings to your cycles long before you need to think about menopause can help you and other women with whom you share your knowledge. You may find that the years before perimenopause are full of clues to its onset. Making notes of your experiences also helps you learn to listen to your body. A calendar devoted to this effort is an efficient and simple way to keep your records.

On the calendar, make notes of your physical changes and use an "X" to denote the days of the month when you have your period. If you have any noticeable symptoms, jot down when they appear and rate their severity. Of particular interest are symptoms such as:

> Breast tenderness
>
> Yearning for sweets
>
> Swelling, bloating
>
> Headaches
>
> Depressed feelings
>
> Increased sexual desire
>
> Increased energy
>
> Decreased energy
>
> Feelings of anger
>
> General mood swings

This information may also provide the clues to help you and your doctor determine whether or which hormone replacement protocol may be best for you when you are ready to make that decision.

The entire question of what information to pull together for your daughter might be best defined if you think about what you wish your mother had told you. How old was she when she first became aware she was experiencing hormonal

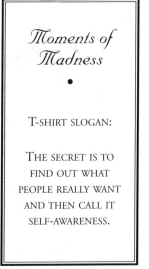

Moments of Madness

•

T-SHIRT SLOGAN:

THE SECRET IS TO FIND OUT WHAT PEOPLE REALLY WANT AND THEN CALL IT SELF-AWARENESS.

shifts? What tipped her off? How did she feel? How did she cope? What remedied the situation for her?

CHARTING THE FAMILY TREE

In addition to understanding more about your mother's adjustment to menopause, learn all you can about the health histories of other relatives. That can be difficult if you're adopted or have had to deal with family breakups or rifts. One of our friends set out to find her birth mother only to learn she really didn't have much to share with this woman. The birth mother, on the other hand, now wants to become the mother she never was. This is adding more stress to our friend's already stressful midlife experience.

If possible, see if you can create a family health tree to share with your children or nieces and nephews. Try to gather as much information as possible about the causes of death and any health problems relatives have had. Significant illnesses might include cancer, heart disease, rheumatoid arthritis, diabetes, or any others that concern you. In some cases, you could provide your family with good clues to ways to prevent future problems.

MADNESS: ANOTHER VIEW

Today there's plenty of evidence that feelings profoundly affect health. For many women, midlife seems to be a time when repressed feelings demand a voice. Suppose you have overlooked annoying habits in your family for a years—say sloth, for example. Your family refuses any responsibility for housekeeping or maintaining a healthy environment. Without you, the house becomes a garbage dump. And you don't want to put up with it any more!

You can react as one woman—a full-time working mom—did and go on strike. She put a sign on her lawn, announcing her stance. She told the neighbors her home's working conditions were intolerable. The local TV station showed up at her door to film the situation and display the sordid reality on the ten o'clock news. Out of embarrassment, her husband and kids agreed to work harder to carry their share of the load.

Here's one thing medical science is learning: Never endure in silence for any longer than you have to. Repressed feelings, especially madness, or anger, can be hazardous to your long-term health. That does not mean you have the right to mercilessly cut others down because they annoy you. Nor does it give you the right to become physically abusive to others. It does mean you need to be aware of the things that trigger intense anger or frustration.

Once you know your triggers, it helps to make a list of alternative ways to handle them. Talking about specific situations helps many women, and while this may make you think "therapy," it could mean "support group" as well. The point is, don't store up anger in your body! Find a way to let it out! Anger, no less than toxic waste, does terrible physical damage over the course of a lifetime. And it seems the body never forgets.

Emotions have a definite effect on the immune system. When you're happy, your immune system kicks into high gear and fights off infections, helps your joints operate smoothly, improves your digestion, and helps you sleep more peacefully. People who are happy and in touch with their emotions seem to have more energy and to live longer. Look at George Burns, Bob Hope, and Phyllis Diller. Laughter is apparently good medicine.

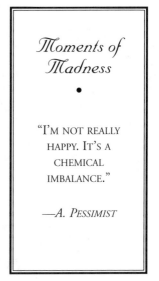

Moments of Madness

•

"I'M NOT REALLY HAPPY. IT'S A CHEMICAL IMBALANCE."

—*A. Pessimist*

Emotions, we are learning, are neither spontaneous nor mysteriously caused actions. They are reactions to events, thoughts, or experiences. When we have an emotional reaction, physical and chemical changes take place in the body.

When something makes you feel angry or threatened, a series of changes begins in the hypothalamus, one of the key players in the perimenopause. This gland then signals the pituitary, which sends signals to the adrenal glands. The adrenals, already overworked during the time of hormonal changes in the female body, produce chemicals called catecholamines, including adrenaline, which produce physical changes in the entire body. Blood pressure rises, the heart beats faster, hairs all over the body stand at attention, stomach muscles go into spasm, and the blood supply surges and increases to the large muscles. The body is ready for war.

While this sounds complex, it is really basic. The body has only two modes of response: one for war and the other for peace. When we get in touch with our feelings and learn how to promote peace and avoid war, we make our bodies more physically comfortable by avoiding war-making chemicals and increasing the production of the endorphins that make us feel good and calm us down.

In women's bodies, the link between the war-making chemicals and physical discomforts has been documented in cystitis, dysmenorrhea, endometriosis, and sometimes infertility. In more extreme cases, arthritis, cancer, hypertension, and emphysema are also suspect. Some researchers believe that all illness is a manifestation of emotional dis-ease.

This in no way implies that "It's all in your head," as doctors used to tell women who had symptoms of perimenopause. Your feelings are real and important. You have every right to own them and react to them.

What do we do about the inevitable disappointments of life? What of the rejections, the anxieties, the losses? Well, it appears that being aware of the link between your feelings and your health is a good first step toward wellness. Another proactive approach to resolving feelings is to talk about them. Sharing trials with a sympathetic friend or group of friends seems to reduce the pressures on our bodies so we have a chance to become and remain healthier.

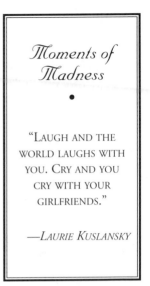

Moments of Madness

•

"LAUGH AND THE WORLD LAUGHS WITH YOU. CRY AND YOU CRY WITH YOUR GIRLFRIENDS."

—*LAURIE KUSLANSKY*

When something sad happens or you feel bad about something, take some action to counteract that feeling. Unexpressed bad feelings cause the body to respond with pain, inflammation, cramps, or a host of other symptoms. Do something that will help you feel better. Every cell in your body is favorably affected and benefits from the good feeling.

Is this true during perimenopause? The fact is it's true all the time—no less during the menopausal years than at other times in a woman's life. But during these years, your emotions are likely to be affected by the hormonal changes in your body. You feel more vulnerable.

Many women report they feel out of control or they cry over insignificant things. Is this normal? You bet. If you have a feeling, express it. Get it out of your system. Granted, some feelings are best expressed in private, so allow yourself time to be alone when you need it.

Luckily, women are more in touch with feelings and don't have to question them as the men in their lives do. When we ask our husbands how they feel, most say something like, "Well, I'm not tired, I'm not hungry, and I don't have to go to

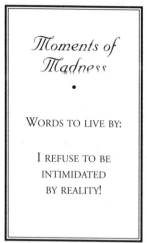

Moments of Madness

•

WORDS TO LIVE BY:

I REFUSE TO BE
INTIMIDATED
BY REALITY!

the bathroom, so I guess I feel fine." As women, we are looking for something far deeper, something that reveals the spiritual, feeling part of our nature. Most men have a hard time understanding that.

Some years ago, the government spent millions of dollars on a study that proved healthy people are happier than sick people. Most of us were outraged at this seemingly ridiculous investment. But the study could have been vindicated if the researchers had asked whether happy people are sick less often than unhappy individuals. And if so, why? While we believe that's true, again we aren't sure which is the chicken and which the egg.

Until we learn more, we'll go out on a limb and say if you want to be happy, have happy experiences. Schedule them into your life. If music gives you joy, get more music into your life. If art is your thing, make it a priority. If you absolutely love to cook, do it. If you can't eat everything you cook, give it away. That will make you feel good, too.

If you want to remain healthy, get to know your feelings—or get in touch with your "inner child." The moment you experience a bad feeling, acknowledge it. Then get rid of it through words, tears, or journal writings or by sharing it with others. Never let negative feelings accumulate inside yourself. When you do, your body does the complaining. And that, along with other symptoms of perimenopause, can create grave challenges to your long-term health.

KEEPING IT IN PERSPECTIVE

The daughter of friends recently sent this letter:

Dear Mom and Dad,

I'm sorry I haven't written, but most of my things were burned up when the sorority house caught fire. I'm out of the hospital now and the doctor says the scarring won't require more than three or four operations. I've moved into the fraternity house next door and am sharing a room with some of the guys who rescued me from the fire.

Oh yes, I know how much you're looking forward to grandchildren, so you should be happy to learn I'm pregnant.

Love,

Courtney

P.S. There was no fire. I'm perfectly fine and not pregnant. In fact, I don't even have a boyfriend. But I did get a D in French and a C in math and chemistry. I just wanted to make sure you'd keep things in perspective.

While the issues in your life during these perimenopausal years are certainly serious and may cause some discomfort and inconvenience, they aren't so serious that they should overshadow other aspects of your life. A healthy dose of fun can go a long way toward helping you to overcome them.

If there is any advice we all want to give our daughters, it's "enjoy your life." The need for reflection and reevaluation that accompany midlife and menopause provides an opportunity for change in more than just your hormone levels. It gives you the chance to loosen up, lighten up, and have more fun.

We remember our last conversation with a dear friend a week before she died of a sudden and totally unexpected ruptured aneurysm. Her major concern that last week of her life was disciplining herself to start yet another diet, since she thought she looked a little flabby. At age 70, she died still trying to look good for others.

Personally, we're choosing to have as much fun as we possibly can in the last weeks of our lives—and in every week before. We've made a commitment to accept our bodies the way they are. That doesn't mean we won't take care of them. But it does mean we won't continually try to reshape ourselves to meet someone else's standards.

We, the Hot Flashers of this world, pledge to wear bright colors and to smile more often; to learn to remember and repeat jokes; to let ourselves cry at the movies; and to help each other with attitude adjustment as needed.

Moments of Madness

•

"THINGS TURN OUT BEST FOR THOSE WHO MAKE THE BEST OF THE WAY THINGS TURN OUT."

We've decided to work hard, but we don't want to forget to play hard, too. Our motto is "Do what you like and like what you do." There's great pleasure in helping people, but there's hardly any fun at all in sitting home alone counting your assets.

So, what started in the ladies' room in Atlanta ended here as a book. There's nothing wrong with a support group that meets in a bathroom, but it's much more fun to meet at New York's Russian Tea Room. Or at the top of the Eiffel Tower. Or in the Waikiki Hilton. What the heck, think big! Head for the ladies' rooms of them all.

Selected
Bibliography

Barbach, Lonnie: *The Pause*. New York: Dutton, 1993.

Beard, Mary and Curtis, Lindsay: *Menopause and the Years Ahead*. Tucson, AZ: Fisher Books, 1991.

Boston Women's Health Book Collective: *The New Our Bodies, Ourselves*. New York: Touchstone, 1992.

Brown, Helen Gurley: *The Late Show*. New York: Wm. Morrow and Co., 1993.

Chinen, Allan B.: *Once Upon a Midlife*. Los Angeles: Jeremy Tarcher, 1992.

Cole-Whittaker, Terry: *Love and Power in a World Without Limits*. San Francisco: Harper and Row Publishers, 1989.

Cone, Faye Kitchener: *Making Sense of Menopause*. New York: Fireside, 1993.

Cutler, Winnifred B.: *Hysterectomy: Before and After*. New York: Harper and Row, 1990.

Dranov, Paula: *Estrogen: Is It Right for You?* New York: Fireside, 1991.

Foley, Denise, and Nechas, Eileen: *Women's Encyclopedia of Health and Emotional Healing*. Emmaus, PA: Rodale Press, 1993.

Friedan, Betty: *The Fountain of Age*. New York: Simon & Schuster, 1993.

Frisch, Melvin: *Stay Cool Through Menopause* New York: The Body Press/ Perigee by Putnam, 1993.

Gillespie, Clark, M.D.: *Hormones, Hot Flashes and Mood Swings*. New York: Harper Collins, 1989.

Gladstar, Rosemary: *Herbal Healing for Women*. New York: Fireside, 1993.

Greer, Germaine: *The Change*. New York: Fawcett Columbine, 1991.

Jacobowitz, Ruth S.: *150 Most-Asked Questions about Menopause*. New York: Hearst Books, 1993.

Jovanovic, Lois, with Levert, Suzanne: *A Woman Doctor's Guide to Menopause*. New York: Hyperion, 1993.

Kahn, Ada P., and Holt, Linda H.: Midlife Health: *A Woman's Guide to Feeling Good*. New York, Avon Books, 1987.

Korte, Diana: *Every Woman's Body*. New York: Fawcett Columbine, 1994.

Landau, Carol, Cyr, Michele G., and Moulton, Anne W.: *The Complete Book of Menopause*. New York: G.P. Putnam's Sons, 1994.

Lu, Henry C.: *Chinese System of Food Cures*. New York: Sterling Publishing Co., 1986.

Nachtigall, Lila E., M.D., and Heilman, Joan Rattner: *Estrogen*. New York: Harper Collins, 1991.

Notelovitz, Morris, M.D., Ph.D., and Tonnessen, Diana: *Menopause and Midlife Health*. New York: St. Martins Press, 1993.

Paige, Judith, and Gordon, Pamela: *Choice Years.* New York: Fawcett Crest, 1991.

Perry, Susan, and O'Hanlan, Katherine: *Natural Menopause.* New York: Addison-Wesley Publishing Co., 1992.

Rush, Martin, M.D.: *Decoding the Secret Language of Your Body.* New York: Fireside, 1994.

Sachs, Judith: *What Women Should Know About Menopause.* New York: Dell Publishing, 1991.

Sand, Gayle: *Is It Hot in Here or Is It Me?* New York: Harper Collins, 1993.

Sheehy, Gail: *The Silent Passage.* New York: Random House, 1991.

Smith, John: *Women and Doctors.* New York: Dell,1992.

Stewart, Felicia, Guest, Felicia, Stewart, Gary, and Hatcher, Robert A.: *Understanding Your Body: Every Woman's Guide to Gynecology and Health,* New York, Bantam Books, 1987.

Trien, Susan Flamholtz: *The Menopause Handbook.* New York: Ballantine Books, 1986.

Utian, Wulf, and Jacobowitz, Ruth: *Managing Your Menopause.* New York: Fireside, 1990.

Weed, Susun S.: *Menopausal Years.* Woodstock, NY: Ash Tree Publishing, 1992.

Weiss, M.D., Robert, and Subak-Sharpe, Genell: *Complete Guide to Health and Well-Being After 50,* Columbia University School of Public Health, Times Books, 1988.

INDEX

abdominal bloating, 134
abdominal hysterectomy, 150
ACE, 91
aching joints and muscles, 25
acne, 26, 27, 65, 165
acupuncture, 26, 140
adolescence, 27
adrenal glands, 2, 14, 15, 52, 93, 115, 230
adrenal system, 140
adrenaline, 32, 72, 230
Advil, 68, 111
African-Americans, 152
aging and food, 200
alcohol
    and breast cancer, 128
    and dizziness, 62
    and hormones, 128
Aldactone, 92
allergic reactions, 9
allergies, 28, 31, 115
allergy testing, 29
alternative physicians, 31
alternative therapies, 171
Alzheimer's disease, 192
American College of
    Obstetricians and
    Gynecologists, 166
American Fertility Society, 126, 189
American Heart Association, 48, 126, 189
American Medical Association, Journal of, 39
Anatomy of an Illness, 219
androgen measurements, 111
androgens, 103, 105, 142, 165
androgens, side effects of, 165
Android/Testred/Oreton, 142
anemia, 155

anger, 6
angina, 191
angiotensin-converting enzyme, 91
ankylosing spondylitis, 219
anovulation, 113
antibiotics, 123
antidepressants, 57, 65, 72, 96
antihistamines, 30, 65
antihypertensives, 65, 96
antioxidants, 138, 201
antispasmodic drug, 138
antiviral agents, 72
anxiety, 31, 33, 102, 161
arteriosclerotic heart disease, 141
arthritis, 29, 114, 206, 230
aspirin, 82
Astroglide, 195
atherosclerosis, 90, 133
atherosclerotic heart disease, 85
atrophic vaginitis, 108, 126
autogenic dysregulation, 46
autoimmune diseases, 29
Aygestin,143

backaches, 11, 25
bad breath, 34
balloon angioplasty, 191
behavior modification, 122
Bellergal, 89, 105, 138
beta blockers, 91
beta carotene, 27, 201, 202
beta-adrenergic blockers, 83
beta-estradiol, 142
bethanechol, 98
Bible, 219
bilateral oophorectomy, 150
bilateral salpingo-oophorectomy, 149

biofeedback training, 102
bioflavonoids, 102
black cohosh, 138
blackheads, 27
bladder
    cancers, 151
    changes, 36
    disease, 136
    infections, 36
    problems, 140
    training, 98
bleeding, 40, 74, 85
blood cholesterol, 115
blood clots, 191
blood pressure, 130, 172, 215, 230
blood sugar, 33, 141
bonding, dental, 55
bone density scan, 41
bone loss, 9, 16, 41
bone problems, 40
boron, 138
Boston Collaborative Drug Surveillance Study, 127
BRAIDED concept, 159
brain function and estrogen, 45
brain static, 46
breakthrough bleeding, 134
breast
    cancer, 43, 118, 127, 129, 131-133, 163, 174; 190, 216
    changes, 42
    exam, 43, 172
    pain, 134
    risk assessment, 176
Bristol Myers, 142
Brooks, Theodore, 107
burning mouth, 43
Burns, George, 229
buttonhole operation, 61
buzzing sound, 45

caesarean section, 148
caffeine, 70
calcium, 16, 40, 54, 138, 188, 208
    channel blockers, 91
    deficiency, 25
    sources of, 209
    supplements, 39
Caltrate, 600 42
cancer, 114, 174, 230
    see also specific types, such as breast
candida albicans, 123
capsaicin, 210
cardiopulmonary problems, 162
cardiovascular disease, 87, 91, 126, 163, 164, 188-192
Carnick Amen, 142
carpal tunnel syndrome, 6, 46, 47
cataract, 63
catecholamines, 56, 103, 230
cavities, 64
CBC, 111
Center for Health Statistics, 162
cervical cancer, 181, 211
cervical polyps, 108
CFS, 71
chest pain and pressure, 47
    see also heart palpitations
chills, 48, 88
chlamydia, 111
chlorotrianisene, 142
cholesterol, 86, 87,140, 173,
chronic fatigue, 71, 115
chronic infections, 115
chronic pelvic pain, 158
Ciba-Geigy, 142
circulation, 140
climacteric, 5
Clonidine, 89, 105, 138

collagen, 28, 81, 96
collagen injections ,97
colon cancer, 151
color Doppler ultrasound, 108
Columbia University College of
    Physicians and Surgeons, 193
complete blood cell count, 111
complete hysterectomy, 149
compression of morbidities, 2
conjugated estrogens, 15, 143
constipation, 74, 162
contraindications for hormone
    replacement therapy, 132
coronary angiography, 191
coronary artery disease, 85,
    172, 191
corpus luteum, 12, 14
cortisol, 115
coumarins, 210
Cousins, Norman, 219
cramping, menstrual, 68
cramps, foot and leg, 25, 49
    see also aching joints
    and muscles
crawling skin, 77
cross-linkage theory, 200
crying jag, xi, 51
Cushing's syndrome, 93
Cycrin, 143
cystitis, 36, 230

Danacrin, 111
DDT, 175
decreased sexual desire, 52
Delestrogen, 143
dental bonding, 55
dental problems, 53, 64
dentist, 35
Depo-Estradiol, 143
Depo-Testadiol, 143
depressed immune function,
    115

depression, 6, 11, 55, 102, 103,
    114, 116, 134, 141, 161, 162
    and diet, 56
    and exercise, 56
    and libido, 52
dermatologist, 27
desire to be alone, 58
DHE, 83
diabetes 37, 57, 169, 191, 202,
    206
diabetic retinopathy, 64
dienestro, 142, 143
diet and anxiety, 33
diet and cholesterol, 87
diet and depression, 56
diet and gallbladder disease, 60
Diethylstilbestrol suppositories,
    142
digestive distresses, 59, 78
    see also gastric upset
dihydro-ergotamine, 83
dilation and curettage, 69, 74,
    86, 108, 155
Diller, Phyllis, 229
Dimetapp, 98
Disalcid, 83
disorientation, 6
Ditropan, 98
diuretics, 91
dizziness, 6, 61, 62, 150
dong quai, 89, 138
Doppler sonograms, 179
dry eyes, 63
dry mouth, 64
dry skin, 65
Duke Center for the Study
    of Aging and Human
    Development, 107
Duke University, 194
Duvivier Risk Assessment
    Profiles, 176, 178, 180, 182,
    184

dysfunctional uterine bleeding, 154
dysmenorrhea, 230

edema, 165
elasticity of bladder, 38
elastin, 28
electrocoagulation, 154
electrocardiography (ECG), 173, 190
electrodessication, 155
electroencephalogram, 102
electrolysis, 92
electrolyte imbalances, 84
Elisabeth Kubler-Ross, 80
emotional swings, 16
emotional upheaval, see mood swings
emphysema, 230
endocrine glands, 48
endocrine system and stress, 114
endocrinopathy, 3
endometrial ablation, 155
endometrial cancer, 108, 128, 133, 163, 178
endometrial hyperplasia, 69, 108
endometrial sampling, 86, 108, 174
Endometriosis Association, 167
endometriosis, 133, 150, 151, 153, 154, 230
endometrium, 14
endorphins, 117
EPART, 136
erratic menstruation, 67
erythromycin, 123
esterified estrogens, 143
Estinyl, 143
Estovis, 142

Estrace, 98, 142
Estraderm, 98, 142
estradiol, 12, 15, 143
estradiol cypionate, 143
estradiol valerate, 143
Estratab, 143
Estraval intramuscular parenteral estrogen, 143
Estregard Cream, 143
estrogen
  and PMS, 110
  and prolapse, 158
  cream, 118
  deficient states, 1
  patch, 142
  scare, 126
  side effects of, 134
  vaginal insert, 119
estrogen-progestogen-androgen replacement therapy, 136
estrone, 12, 121
estropipate, 142
exercise, 17
  and depression, 56
  and water retention,122
  stress tests, 190
extracerebral vasodilation, 82
eyes, 63, 172
eyesight, 63, 194

fallopian tubes, 150
family tree, 228
fatigue, 10, 70, 162
fats in food, 203
fear, 72
  see also anxiety
fecal impaction, 96
fecal occult blood test, 173
Female Patient, The, 107
Femtrol, 89, 105, 138
fiber, 204

fibrinogen, 130
fibroids, 69, 74, 86, 133, 148, 150, 151
flavonoids, 210
flavoxate, 98
fluid retention, 119, 134
flushing, 75, 105, 163
see also heart palpitations, hot flashes
follicle stimulating hormone, 12, 13, 14, 60, 61, 67, 68, 86, 111, 114
follicles, 81
Food and Drug Administration, 125
food and aging, 200
foot and leg cramps, 25, 49
forgetfulness, 102
formication, 77
Framingham Heart Study, 122, 158
free-radical theory, 200
frequent urination,
see loss of urinary control

Gabrielson, Jo, 207
gallbladder disease, 60, 79
gallstones, 60, 61, 134, 136
Gambrell, Dr. R. Don, 127, 128
gamma globulin, 72
gastric upset, 78
gastric upset, see also digestive distresses
gastrointestinal upset, 59
gelotology, 219
genistein, 211
genital prolapse, 151, 156
genital self-examination, 109
Gerontology Research Center, 205, 206

gingivitis, 34
gingivitis and birth control pills 35
gingivitis and pregnancy, 35
ginseng, 89, 105, 139
glaucoma, 63
Goldwater Memorial Hospital, 127
gonadotropin-releasing hormone agonists 111, 152
Graduate Hospital, 165
grief, 51, 79, 80
Grief Observed, A, 134grief, see also depression
gum disease, 34, 54, 64

hair growth, 92
hair loss 2, 81
and hormonal imbalance, 81
halitosis, 34
Hanimine, 98
hardening of the arteries, 133
headaches, 6, 11, 82, 134, 140
health care team, selecting, 169
heart attack, 10, 90, 158
heart disease, 16, 114, 126, 133, 140, 188
heart palpitations, 10, 84
see also chest pain, flushing, and hot flashes
heavy bleeding, 74, 85
hemorrhage, 162
HERS Foundation, 166
high blood pressure, 76, 90, 114, 138, 205, 230
high cholesterol, 86, 206
high density lipoproteins (HDL), 87, 91, 130, 188
hijiki, 95
histamine blockers.,72
homeopathics, 30, 31, 140

Hope, Bob, 229
hormonal imbalances and hair
  loss, 81
hormone additive therapy, 26
hormone replacement therapy
  about 125-143
  and anxiety, 33
  and bone loss, 41
  and breast changes, 43
  and crying jags, 51
  and dry eyes, 63
  and fear of being alone in
    public, 73
  and fibroids, 74
  and flushing, 76
  and headaches, 82
  and heart palpitations, 85
  and hypertension, 91
  and memory loss, 100
  and mood swings, 104
  and night sweats, 105
  and spotting, 113
  and weight gain, 121
  costs of, 141
  contraindications, 132
  stopping, 135
hot flashes, xi, 6, 7, 9, 14, 47,
  48, 75, 84, 88, 105, 119,
  138, 150, 163, 196
  see also flushing
    and heart palpitations
humor, 8, 217
humor psychology, 219
Hutchins, Francis L., 165
hydrochloric acid, 59
hypertension, 90, 138, 230
hypertension and hormone
  replacement therapy, 91
hypertrichologist, 92
hyperventilation, 62
hypothalamic-pituitary-ovarian
  cycle, 68

hypothalamus, 12, 13, 14, 48,
  58, 77, 129, 230
Hysterectomy Educational
  Resource and Services, 106
hysterectomy, 11, 69, 75, 111,
  145-167
  abdominal, 147
  complete, 149
  emotions and, 161
  frequency of, 148
  radical, 149
  subtotal, 149
  total, 149
  who needs, 151
hysteroscopic endometrial
  ablation, 155
hysteroscopic techniques, 153
hysteroscopy, 74, 108
Hytrin, 98

ICN Pharm, 142
imipramine, 98
Imitrex, 83
immune system, 10, 37, 211,
  217
immune system and stress, 114
immune theory, 200
immune-system blockers, 72
incontinence, 36, 74, 96
increased hair growth, 92
increased sexual desire, 93
Inderal, 83
indoles, 211
infection, 151
infertility, 74, 230
inflammation of bladder, 37
  of joints, 29
inflammatory lesions of face, 27
inner ear disturbance, 62
insomnia, 70, 94, 102, 119
Institute for Reproductive
  Health 167

insulin, 130, 215
  resistance, 199
intramural fibroids, 152
intramuscular injections, 136
invasive cancer, 151
iron deficiency, 69
irrigators, 36
irritability, 6, 70, 102
  see also mood swings
isolation, 58
isothiocyanates, 211
itching skin 77
  vaginal, 118

Janimine, 98
Jenny Craig, 122
joint inflammation, 29
joint pain, 6, 25
  in chronic fatigue syndrome,
    71
*Journal of the American Medical
  Association,* 39

K-Y jelly, 195
Kegel exercises, 39, 96, 97, 98,
  157
kelp, 95
kidney obstruction, 37
kidney problems, 172
Klein, Barbara, 194
Koop, C. Everett, 202

lack of sexual desire, 52
laparoscope, 151
laparoscopic cholescystectomy,
  61, 78
laparoscopic techniques, 153
laparoscopically assisted
  laser surgery, 154
  vaginal hysterectomy
    (LAVH), 151
Lee, John R., 163, 164

leg cramps, 49, 138
leiomyomas, 74, 152
Levy, Barbara, 159
libido, loss of, 52
licorice, 138
lignins, 211
Lilly, 142
liver, 59, 77, 165
liver disorders, 132
liver enzymes, 111
loss of urinary control, 96
  see also bladder changes
lost-lust syndrome, 136
low blood pressure, 49
low blood sugar, 115
low-density lipoprotein (LDL),
  87, 90, 91, 130, 188, 201
lupus, 29
luteinizing hormone (LH), 12,
  13, 14, 60, 61, 68, 86, 111
lycopene, 211
lymph glands in CFS, 71

mammography, 43, 173, 174
manic-depressive illness, 116
marijuana, 52
massage therapy, 26
Mayo Clinic Health Letter, 218
Mead Johnson, 142
Medical College of Georgia,
  127, 128
meditation, 70, 140
medroxyprogesterone acetate,
  142, 143
Megace, 142
megesterol acetate, 142
melatonin, 95
memory loss, 2, 6, 98
menarche, 2
menopause symptoms journal,
  224
menopause information gap, 2

Mensi/Menopause
   questionnaire, 22
menstruation, 2, 5
mental fuzziness, 45, 100
mental illness, 7
mental static, 45
Merrill-Dow, 142
methyl testosterone, 143
micronized estradiol, 142
Micronor, 142
migraine headaches, 82, 84
   see also headaches
Minipress, 98
minoxidil, 81
mitral valve prolapse (MVP), 48
Monistat, 124
monoamine oxidase (MAO),
   103
monosodium glutamate, 28, 82
mood swings, 11, 82, 102, 104,
   141
Motrin® 111
mouth changes, 44
MSG, 28
multivitamins, 140
muscle pain, 6, 25
muscle weakness in chronic
   fatigue syndrome, 71
myalgia, 25
myomas, 74
myomectomy, 75, 153

Nachtigall study, 127
naproxen sodium, 83
National Cancer Institute, 175
National Center for Health
   Statistics, 149
National Institute of Aging,
   205, 206
National Institute of Health,
   90, 130, 139

National Women's Health
   Resource Center, 159, 161,
   166
*Natural Progesterone: The
   Multiple Roles of a Remarkable
   Hormone,* 163
nausea, 104, 134
   see also digestive distresses
negative thinking,
   see depression and mood
   swings
nervous system, 140
nervousness, 72, 114, 134
nervousness, see anxiety,
   mood swings, and stress
Newman, Paul, 199
nifedipine, 98
night sweats, 6, 9, 14, 94, 105,
   150, 196
nonmalignant tumors, 86
nonsteroidal anti-inflammatory
   drugs (NSAIDs), 83, 111
Nor-Q.D., 143
norethindrone, 142, 143
norgestrol, 143
Norlutate, 142
Norlutin, 142
Nuprin, 68
Nurses' Health Study, 78
Nystatin, 124

oatmeal, 140
obesity, 202
OBG Management, 24
Office of Alternative Medicine,
   90
Ogen, 142
On Death and Dying, 80
oophorectomy, defined, 149
oral contraceptives, 35, 155
oral estrogen, 142

oral hygiene, 35
Ortho, 142
Ortho Dienestrol Cream, 142
orthopedist, 169
osteoporosis, 16, 17, 25, 35,
    54, 106, 126, 132, 133,
    141, 159, 163, 164, 169,
    183-188
ovarian cancer, 180
ovarian cysts, 114
overflow incontinence, 96
Ovrette, 143
ovulation, 14, 67
ovulation and headaches, 82
oxidative cell damage, 201
oxybutynin, 98
oxygen metabolism, 200
ozone, 200

pain with intercourse, 106
pancreas, 15
panic attacks, see anxiety
Pap smear, 109, 173
parenteral estrogen, 143
Park-Davis, 142
partial hysterectomy, 149
PCB, 175
pelvic
    inflammatory disease
        (PID), 111
    pain, 74
    sonogram, 86
    ultrasound, 108
penicillin, 123
PEPI Trial, 130
peptic ulcers, 114
periodontal disease, 34
personal health management
    program, 172
pessary, 97, 156
phenylpropanolamine, 98
photovaporization, 155

phytochemicals, 210
phytoestrogens, 138, 210
pineal gland, 15
pituitary, 13, 14, 15, 58, 67,
    121
pituitary tumors, 84
plaque, 34, 54
PMS, 34, 110, 163
polybrominated biphenyls
    (PBB), 175
polycystic ovarian disease, 93
polyps, 86
post-partum blues, 56, 57
Postel, 68
postmenopausal
    estrogen/progestin
        interventions trial, 130
    vaginal bleeding, 107
potassium, 91
    bicarbonate, 187
power surge, 75, 89
prazosin, 98
pregnancy, 2, 27, 113
Premarin, 98, 143
    vaginal cream, 143
premature ovarian failure, 163
premenstrual syndrome, 34,
    110
Procardia, 98
progesterone
    and PMS, 110
    side effects of, 134
progestin, 142
prolactin, 111
propranolol, 83
prostacyclins, 158
prostaglandin, 159
Provera, 143
Proverbs, 219
Prozac, 33
pseudephedrine, 98
psychoactive drugs, 111

Psychological Science, 216
psychology of humor, 219
pulmonary embolism, 132

quinestrol, 142

radical hysterectomy, 149
rage, 114
    see also depression, grief,
    and stress
Raines, Claude, 100
Ravdin, Peter, 128
reconstructive surgery
    for prolapse, 157
rectum, cancer of, 151
Redford, Robert, 199
Rejuvex, 89, 105, 138, 195
respiratory symptoms, 29
Retin-A, 27
retirement, 32
rheumatoid arthritis, 29, 64
risk assessment,
    cervical cancer, 182
    endometrial cancer, 178
    osteoporosis, 184
    ovarian cancer, 180
    uterine cancer, 178
Rockefeller University, 45, 101
Rogaine, 81

s-allycysteine, 211
salpingo-oophorectomy, 149
Sarrel, Phillip, 21
Schering, 143
sebaceous glands, 65
sedatives, 137
Seldane, 30
selenium, 138, 201, 202
Selye, Hans, 217
serotonin, 56, 117
serotonin and PMS, 110

sex
    and aging, 194
    after hysterectomy, 165
sexual desire
    changes in, 6, 52
    increased, 93
sexually transmitted diseases,
    182
Shadowland, 80
sigmoidoscopy, 173
sinus infections, 35
skin cancer, 173
skin sensitivities, 77
sleep deprivation, 70
sleep disturbances, 56, 70, 94
    102, 119
smoking, 17
sodium bicarbonate, 187
sodium fluoride, 188
Solvay, 143
sore breasts, 42
    see also breast changes
sore throat, 71
spironolactone, 92
spotting, 68, 113
Squibb, 143
State University of New York,
    39
stress, 114, 138, 217
stress incontinence, 74, 96
stress response, 115
stress vitamins, 80
stroke, 90, 158, 172, 188
submucosal fibroids, 152
subserous fibroids, 152
subtotal hysterectomy, 149
Sudafed, 98
suicidal thoughts,
    see depression and stress
Sumatriptan, 83
support groups, xii, 161, 229

supracervical hysterectomy, 149
surgeon general, 202
surgical menopause, 149
Syntex, 143

Tace, 142
Tamoxifen, 129
tartar, 55
teeth, 34, 141
terazosin, 98
testosterone, 52, 93
testosterone cypionate, 143
thromboembolic disorders, 132
thyroid, 15, 49, 76, 84, 86,
    111, 114, 169
timolol, 83
Tofranil, 98
total hysterectomy, 149
tranquilizers, 52, 137
transdermal patches, 136, 142
transvaginal sonography, 174
triglyceride, 115
triterpenoids, 211
tryptophan, 95, 117
Tums, 42

U.S. Bureau of the Census
    147-148
Understanding Hysterectomy, 166
unilateral oophorectomy, 149
Upjohn, 143
Urecholine, 98
urethra, inflammation of, 37
urethritis, 36
urge incontinence, 96
urinary incontinence, 156
    see also bladder changes
urinary tract, 2
    infections, 36, 162
urine culture, 38
Urispas, 98
uterine bleeding, 151

uterine cancer, 69, 125, 63,
    178,
uterine fibroids, 74
uterine prolapse, 97, 156
Utian, Wulf, 18

vagina, inflammation of, 37
vaginal creams, 137
vaginal dryness, 6, 106, 118,
    140, 150
vaginal itching, 118
vaginal hysterectomy, 150
vaginal keratosis, 165
vaginal tissue health, 194
valerate, 143
valerian, 139
Valium, 137
vasoconstrictors, 83
vasomotor changes, 47, 48, 84,
    88, 126
vision, 63, 194
vitamin A, 27, 28, 65, 201
vitamin B, 39, 65, 80, 138
vitamin B$_6$, 34
vitamin B$_{12}$, 72
vitamin C, 39, 102, 138, 201,
    202, 219
vitamin D, 40, 42, 65
vitamin E, 26, 27, 28, 65, 89,
    102, 138, 201
vulvar cancer, 109

waste products theory, 200
water retention, 42, 119
Waterpik, 54
weakness, 70
    see also fatigue
Weight Watchers, 122, 207
weight changes, 114
weight gain, 6, 120
weight, table of ranges, 206
whiteheads, 27

Women's Health Initiative, 131
Wyeth-Ayerst, 143

x-rays, 35
Xanax, 33

Yale School of Medicine, 21
yeast infections ,123
yoga, 73, 91

zits, 27, 27, 65, 165

CHRONIMED PUBLISHING
BOOKS OF RELATED INTEREST

Fight Fat and Win, Updated & Revised Edition by Elaine Moquette-Magee, R.D., M.P.H. This breakthrough book explains how to easily incorporate low-fat dietary guidelines into every modern eating experience, from fast food and common restaurants to quick meals at home, simply by making smarter choices.

004244   ISBN 1-56561-047-4 $9.95   ❏

Fight Fat & Win Cookbook by Elaine Moquette-Magee, M.P.H., R.D. Now you can give up fat and create great tasting foods without giving up your busy lifestyle. Born from the bestseller *Fight Fat & Win*, this practical cookbook shows you how to make more than 150 easy and tempting snacks, breakfasts, lunches, dinners, and desserts that your family will never know contain little or no fat.

004254   ISBN 1-56561-055-5 $12.95   ❏

Fast Food Facts, Revised and Expanded Edition by Marion Franz, R.D., M.S. This revised and up-to-date best-seller shows how to make smart nutrition choices at fast food restaurants—and tells what to avoid. Includes complete nutrition information of more than 1,500 menu offerings from the 37 largest fast food chains.

Standard-size edition, 004240   ISBN 1-56561-043-1 $7.95   ❏
Pocket edition, 004228   ISBN 1-56561-031-8 $4.95   ❏

Convenience Food Facts by Arlene Monk, R.D., C.D.E., with an introduction by Marion Franz, R.D., M.S. Includes complete nutrition information, tips, and exchange values on more than 1,500 popular name brand processed foods commonly found in grocery store freezers and shelves. Helps you plan easy-to-prepare, nutritious meals.

004081   ISBN 0-937721-77-8 $10.95   ❏

The Brand-Name Guide to Low-Fat and Fat-Free Foods by J. Michael Lapchick with Rosa Mo, R.D., Ed.D. For the first time in one easy-to-swallow guide is a compendium of just about every brand-name food available containing little or no fat—with complete nutrition information.

004242   ISBN 1-56561-045-8 $9.95   ❏

366 Low-Fat Brand-Name Recipes in Minutes by M.J. Smith, M.S., R.D./L.D. Here's more than a year's worth of the fastest family favorites using the country's most popular brand-name foods—from Minute Rice® to Ore Ida®—while reducing unwanted calories, fat, salt, and cholesterol.

004247   ISBN 1-56561-050-4 $12.95   ❏

All-American Low-Fat Meals in Minutes by M.J. Smith R.D., L.D., M.A. Filled with tantalizing recipes and valuable tips, this cookbook makes great-tasting low-fat foods a snap for holidays, special occasions, or everyday. Most recipes take only minutes to prepare.

004079   ISBN 0-937721-73-5 $12.95   ❏

60 Days of Low-Fat, Low-Cost Meals in Minutes by M.J. Smith, R.D., L.D., M.A. Following the path of the best-seller *All American Low-Fat Meals in Minutes*, here are more than 150 quick and sumptuous recipes complete with the latest exchange values and nutrition facts for lowering calories, fat, salt, and cholesterol. This book contains complete menus for 60 days and recipes that use only ingredients found in virtually any grocery store—most for a total cost of less than $10.

004205   ISBN 1-56561-010-5 $12.95   ❏

Muscle Pain Relief in 90 Seconds by Dale Anderson, M.D. Now you're only 90 seconds away from relieving your muscle pain—drug free! From back pain and shin splints to headaches and tennis elbow, Dr. Anderson's innovative "Fold and Hold" technique can help. Simple, safe, and painless, this method is a must for all of us with muscle aches and twinges.

004257   ISBN 1-56561-058-X $10.95   ❏

Taking the Work Out of Working Out by Charles Roy Schroeder, Ph.D. This breakthrough guide shows how to easily convert what many consider to be a chore into enjoyable, creative, and sensual experiences that you'll look forward to. Includes methods for every form of exercise—including aerobics, weight lifting, jogging, dance, and more!
•A Doubleday Health Book Club Selection

004246   ISBN 1-56561-049-0 $9.95   ❏

The Business Traveler's Guide to Good Health on the Road edited by Karl Neumann, M.D., and Maury Rosenbaum. This innovative guide shows business travelers how to make smart food choices, exercise in planes, trains, automobiles, and hotel rooms, relieve stress, and more. Plus, this guide has a listing of hotels in the U.S. and Canada with fitness facilities. All this, presented with a generous seasoning of fun and interesting facts and tidbits, makes the book a must for every business traveler's expense list.

004233   ISBN 1-56561-036-9 $12.95   ❏

The Healthy Eater's Guide to Family & Chain Restaurants by Hope S. Warshaw, M.M.Sc., R.D. Here's the only guide that tells you how to eat healthier in over 100 of America's most popular family and chain restaurants. It offers complete and up-to-date nutrition information and suggests which items to choose and avoid.

004214   ISBN 1-56561-017-2 $9.95   ❑

Fat Is Not a Four-Letter Word by Charles Roy Schroeder, Ph.D. Through interesting scientific, nutritional, and historical evidence, this controversial and insightful guide shows why millions of "overweight" people are unnecessarily knocking themselves out to look like fashion models. It offers a realistic approach to healthful dieting and exercise.

004095   ISBN 1-56561-000-8 $14.95   ❑

Exchanges for All Occasions by Marion Franz, R.D., M.S. Exchanges and meal planning suggestions for just about any occasion, sample meal plans, special tips for people with diabetes, and more.

004201   ISBN 1-56561-005-9 $12.95   ❑

Beyond Alfalfa Sprouts & Cheese: The Healthy Meatless Cookbook by Judy Gilliard and Joy Kirkpatrick, R.D., includes creative and savory meatless dishes using ingredients found in just about every grocery store. It also contains helpful cooking tips, complete nutrition information, and the latest exchange values.

004218   ISBN 1-56561-020-2 $12.95   ❑

One Year of Healthy, Hearty, & Simple One-Dish Meals by Pam Spaude and Jan Owan-McMenamin, R.D., is a collection of 365 easy-to-make healthy and tasty family favorites and unique creations that are meals in themselves. Most of the dishes take under 30 minutes to prepare.

004217   ISBN 1-56561-019-9 $12.95   ❑

Foods to Stay Vibrant, Young & Healthy by Audrey C. Wright, M.S., R.D., Sandra K. Nissenberg, M.S., R.D., and Betsy Manis, R.D. From tips on increasing bone strength to losing weight, here's everything women in midlife need to know to keep young and healthy through food. With authoritative advice from three of the country's leading registered dietitians, women over 40 can eat their way to good health and feel better than ever!

004256   ISBN 1-56561-057-1 $11.95   ❑

200 Kid-Tested Ways to Lower the Fat in Your Child's Favorite Foods by Elaine Moquette-Magee, M.P.H., R.D. For the first time ever, here's a much needed and asked for guide that gives easy, step-by-step instructions to cutting the fat in the most popular brand-name and homemade foods kids eat every day—without them even noticing.

004231   ISBN 1-56561-034-2 $12.95   ❑

Chronimed Publishing
P.O. Box 59032
Minneapolis, Minnesota 55459-9686

Place a check mark next to the book(s) you would like sent. Enclosed is
$ _____. (Please add $3.00 to this order to cover postage and handling. Minnesota residents add 6.5% sales tax.)

Send check or money order, no cash or C.O.D.'s. Prices and availability are subject to change without notice.

Name_____

Address_____

City _____State _____Zip_____

Allow 4 to 6 weeks for delivery.

Quantity discounts available upon request.

Or order by phone: 1-800-848-2793,

612-546-1146 (Minneapolis/St. Paul metro area).

Please have your credit card number ready.